Echoes from the Elands

Cindy Oberholzer

BALBOA.
PRESS
A DIVISION OF HAY HOUSE

Balboa Press books may be ordered through booksellers or by contacting:

Balboa Press
A Division of Hay House
1663 Liberty Drive
Bloomington, IN 47403
www.balboapress.com
1 (877) 407-4847

Print information available on the last page.

ISBN: 978-1-9822-3025-8 (sc)
ISBN: 978-1-9822-3026-5 (e)

Balboa Press rev. date: 06/26/2019

This book is dedicated to Danie Ferreira, who had the forsight to document the happenings in the Elands River Valley. (Uitenhage, South Africa.)

This book is a compilation of stories and poems written and retold by the locals and put together by Cindy Oberholzer.

Contents

1. Elands River Road.. 1
2. The Bull - Halladale Goodluck.. 5
3. Did you know? 6
4. Alan The Chemist.. 6
5. The Grape Story. 7
6. The Jew and the Marbles. 12
7. The Rose and Shamrock.. 12
8. The Hero of Delville Wood – Lukas Gouws. 13
9. Did you know? 16
10. Drought.. 17
11. The "Gullible" Eavesdropper.. 18
12. Did you know? 19
13. Ivan's Story. 19
14. Try Remembering This! 21
15. My Worldly Possessions.. 24
16. Did you know? 24
17. Reaction from Our Farmers. 25
18. The Brother-In-Law and The Whippet. 26
19. 1799 – 1812.. 27
20. The First Blacks in the Valley. 28
21. The Love Story.. 28
22. Reminiscing. 29
23. The Money Lender..31
24. Did You Know?.. 32
25. But now That Faithful. 34

26. Party Lines. 36
27. Did you know? 37
28. Building of a Dam. 38
29. Flood. 39
30. Sweet Little Lettie. 41
31. Did you know? 42
32. The "Hellsa" Long Poem. 43
33. Have you ever seen the Cape? 54
34. Never Forget From Where You've Come. 54
35. Did you Know? 57
36. Hard Times – Hard Times. 57
37. Did you Know? 58
38. From the Book. 59
39. Did you Know? 61
40. A Day at School. 61
41. Did you Know? 62
42. Boys will be Boys. 63
43. Did you Know? 64
44. All the Little Schools. 64
45. Did you know? 67
46. The Donkey. 67
47. The Police. 68
48. The Bench in the Church. 69
49. Everyone is Welcome to the Funeral. 71
50. Crackshot. 71
51. The Postman. 73
52. The Mules. 73
53. Did you Know? 75
54. The Honeymoon. 75
55. Hard Times – For the Ants. 76
56. Highlights of Farming. 76
57. A Run in with the Law. 79
58. The Fire. 79
59. The Folks of the Elands River's 70's 80
60. The Aftermath of Burning. 84

61. Heavens – Thank you- We've come a Long Way. 85
62. An Eccentric Person. 85
63. Did you Know? 86
64. Making Fires is Not for "Sissies". 87
65. Wheat, Modernisation and Danger. 87
66. A Career in Jackal Hunting. 90
67. A Slip of the Tongue! 91
68. The Great Flood. 92
69. Aunt Bettie. 93
70. The Ferreira's. 94
71. A Little History. 94
72. The Establishment of Uitenhage and Surrounds. 95
73. The Prices. 96
74. The Names of Places. 97
75. The Natives. 97
76. The Value of Homesteads. 98
77. Relentless Disasters. 99
78. "You only come across Men and Women like the Voortrekkers once in a Lifetime" 102
79. The "Modern" Postal Service. 103
80. Money System. 104
81. The Market. 104
82. Piet – The Hunter. 105
83. The Brothers Who Married the Sisters. 107
84. The Jackal Club. 108
85. My First Day at Brandwag High School. 108
86. Wheat. 109
87. The Ferreira's. 111
88. The Murder. 113
89. Cradock and Graham. 114
90. The Land System. 114
91. The Slave Proclamation. 115
92. Somerset! 115
93. Pay your Debt! 116
94. Mrs. Uys. 117

95. The Church. 118
96. Thinking Back. 119
97. Van Stadens Bridge Jumpers. 120
98. Three-Feet (Jakob) with his Lots to Say. 120
99. The Commando's. 121
100. The Whiteheads of Elands River. 121
101. Keurkloof. 126
102. Mountain View. 128
103. Forest Glade. 138
104. Gumdale. 140
105. The Meadows. 143
106. Medicinal Plants found in the Elands River Valley used by the locals. 145
107. Life on the Farm. 146
108. All The People. 147
109. Stan and Bert. 147
110. The Circle of Life. 154
111. The Sangoma's Powers. 156
112. Believe It or Not. 157
113. The Orphan Child. 159
114. Rokoptel. 159
115. The Lifeline. 160
116. The Spanish Donkeys. 160
117. Poepbang. 161
118. Missing the Moment. 161
119. Believe It or Not. 162
120. After Eight Years. 162
121. My Grand Parents. 164
122. Our World. 165
123. Life. 167
124. Time. 168
125. Un-Understandable? 169
126. Meals! 170
127. Like a Bird. 171
128. We. 172

129. My Parents 173
130. My Dear, Dear Friend! 175
131. Off Too Hospital! 177
132. The Law? 179
133. Crossword Puzzle? 180
134. The Value of Money – 1804. 181
135. The Keurkloof Ghost. 181
136. The Doctor who Nearly Did Not Become a Doctor! 182
137. Interesting Facts about the Wild Life. 183
138. The Arrival. 184
139. Tragedy. 184
140. The Tourists Drama. 185
141. Come Fetch your Ox 186
142. The Snake that nearly Caused Chaos. 186
143. The Ghost that Unspan Oxen. 187
144. The First Settlers in the Lower Parts of the Elands River Valley. 187
145. The Baviaan – iaan. 189
146. Wattle trees in South Africa. 191
147. Letter to a Mother – 14 January 1944. 192
148. Letter to a Mother – 17 January 1944. 195
149. Letter to a Mother – 24 Febuary 1944. 198
150. Letter to a Mother – 15 May 1945. 201
151. Letter to a Mother – 6 January 1946. 204
152. The Lawyers Bill. 206
153. Did you know? 207
154. Elands River. 207
155. Places to Stay & Things to do. 208
156. A Last Word from the Compiler/Editor/Author. 210
157. A Little About the Author. 211
158. Elands River Rainfall - Mark Dodd - Hillingdon 213

1. Elands River Road.

Left Hand Side	*Right Hand Side*
Uncle Freddies	Sasol
	Rocklands Poultry (Feed)
	Rocklands Intermediate School
Channon Cash Store	
	Rapsy Farm
	Silver Linning – The Standers
Herlewig	
	Blouza Township
Wide Horizon	
	Elands River Nursery
	Opportunity Farm
High Ridge	
	Atlas Kloof
	Sonneck
Boshfontein	
	Dell Farm
M.I.F	
	Waverley Hills

---------------Start of the Gravel Road-----------------

Landela Christian Camp	
Off Camber	
	J. Mansfield + Sons
	Monte Vista
The River Cottage	
	Hillingdon – Mark + Lisa Dodd
	Stilgenoeg – Neels + Patsy Kruger

Bosbokram – Mike + Eben Denysschen

Eikenek – Keith + Maria Dodd

Bergplaas

Peerboom Smietniks

Uitkyk

Bulk River Staff Quarters

Theo Crous Bridge

Bulk River Dam ------------------Bulk River

Bulk River Stone House

Afdak

Mpunzi

Old Church

Gumdale – Elno + Susie Whitehead

Mountain View – George + Anneke Whitehead

Forest Glad

Keurkloof – Carstons + Rene Clotze

Burrows – Tinus + Lorraine Vermaak

Ottos Creek – Derick + Michelle Inggs

Tanglewood–Adrian+CindyOberholzer

Sand River Getaway

Cypherfontein - Hilton + Bruno Willard

Die Hoek – Adrian + Cindy Oberholzer

The Island – Adrian + Cindy Oberholzer

Willem Snyman Bridge

Sand River Dam -------------------Sand River

Stefan + Jacolette Wehmeyer

The Meadows – Donavan + Sunell Whitehead

Oaklands

Elandsfontein

Wistaria – Robin & Melanie Volker

Table Mountain

Elandsbosh – Wouter Vermaak

Kwa Zunga Bush Camp

Tip Tree – Ewald Wehmeyer Slanghoek School

Amoungst Mountains

Highwaters – Danie Ferreira

1950 Church

Rose Cottage School

Wheatlands

Klipkraal

Goosen

Witberg

Poplar Grove

Cotswold

Verkeerdedrif

Houtkloof – Adam and Nele

Middelwater

Melkhoutboom – Ralph +Liezel Clotz

Mount Ingwe – Lukas v d Merwe + Sons

Kammievlei – Roelie + Sareta Beer

Elandskroon – Stan + Bert Rudman (Now Beer)

Bergplaas – Retief Pieterser

Grassnek – Lukas v d Merwe + Sons

Patensie

A view over the Elands River Valley.

2. The Bull - Halladale Goodluck.

A Danie Ferreira story translated and retold by Cindy Oberholzer

Oom Pieter Venter from the farm Rooi Nek, which later become Wysteria, came from the Transvaal, were he farmed on a large scale. He bought Rooi Nek from Oom Natie Heyns.

In the Transvaal he farmed with potatoes, sheep and cattle. One year when his potato crop was ready for harvest, the prices had plummeted through the floor. He decided he would rather plough them up, one row at a time and let his sheep and cattle graze on them. As a result he produced the whitest wool in the entire South Africa.

His cows were the best quality and grew huge and fat, so much so, that transporting and selling them became a problem. Case in point, was his sturdy bull, Halladale Goodluck. This bull took up an entire railway car, with no room to move. For the butchers the bull was too big. Ultimately a few hotels got together and decided to buy and share the bull. For months you could order, from any hotel, scrumptious Halladale Goodluck T-bone or Rump steak.

The bull made such and impression that years later I spotted an advert in the Farmers Weekly under - Pigs: "Large White Boar – Halladale Goodluck" for sale.

3. Did you know?

A Danie Ferreira story translated and retold by Cindy Oberholzer

During the 1920's and 30's it was common to see tramps and bums, with bundles of possessions on their backs, coming down the Elands River Road. These tramps were usually Irish, far from their homes. We called them "Irishmens". It was one of these 'tramps' who told my grandfather of a beautiful place back home, in Ireland, which was called Tip Tree. It looked exactly like Slangerhoek Fontein. From that day the family farm has been called "Tip Tree".

4. Alan The Chemist.

A Danie Ferreira poem translated and retold by Cindy Oberholzer

Our Chemist from Metway Pharm
Holds his ground with great calm
His surname is Gaum, his name is Alan
But today he looks the Hell In.

As he stands all day and mixes potions
Day in and out going through the motions
From this and that he makes his concoctions
For coughs and sneezing and convulsions.

For every ailment from which you frustrate
From an itch to a pain in the prostrate
If you feel off, you will get it at Alan
Medicine by the gallon.

For the eyes he has glasses
For the drugs he took classes
But sad is the look on the young ladies facesAs they must take the pill without their mother's traces.

As Alan will tell the ladies for free
The "boyfriends" drink Viagra like tea.

5. The Grape Story.

A Danie Ferreira story translated and retold by Cindy Oberholzer

The Elands River is a beautiful valley surrounded by huge mountains. On the South side is the Stinkhout Mountains, on the Northern side is the Groot Winterhoek and to the West is the Cockscomb Mountains, which form part of the Winterhoek Mountain.

Only 4 x 4's can make the steep downhills into the Shonga Valley, which forms part of the Groendal Dam. Stunning, natural, crystal clear streams, waterfalls and Yellow Wood trees, which stretch up into the sky.

Lookout over the Shonga Valley.

On the occasional weekend, this is where we would go camping, fishing and catching eels. So, you can imagine my shock when on such an occasion we came across a tent tucked away in a small valley. Along with a washing line displaying a pair of panties.

I wanted to take a closer look, however my mates stopped me, so we rode on past. However those damn panties worried me.

My goodness, look at the size of those Eel out the Elands River

We meandered a further 6 or so kilometres deeper into the mountains till we came to our camping spot, at Buffelsgat. As the sun was setting we set up camp, fished, made a fire, braaied and caught eel. I obvioully caught the biggest eel, as thick as my upper arm. On either side of Buffelsgat were sheer cliffs that extended up into the clouds. The silence consumed us. Little stones dropped off the cliff into the pond, one by one. No doubt a leopard restlessly patrolled above us, on the cliff tops.

When all of a sudden, a person appeared from out of the darkness and came and stood next to me. "My Boss, the Missies from up there asks if my boss has a few cigarettes for her?" he stammered. My cigarette pack was open, which was half full. Out of sheer shock I gave him my half box, as I had another. Just as he appeared from the darkness, so did he disappear into the darkness.

I did not sleep well that night thinking of this isolated world, my half a box of smokes and those damn panties on the line.

The weekend was over so we packed up and began our journey home. We once again passed the washing line, this time no panties in sight. We stopped and I called out "Hello, anyone home?" To my suprise an absolutely gorgeous young women appeared from out the tent. Ah – the owner of the panties. She introduced herself and invited me into the tent. What I saw left me dumbstruck – cases and cases of grapes, packed to the ceiling of the tent. On one side between even more cases of grapes, lay a man, on a camp bed. Even at a glance one could see he was extremely sick. He was just skin and bone, his cheeks were sunken in and he could barely lift his arms or speak.
She went on to tell me her husband was suffering from an incurable terminal illness and out of sheer desperation she took the advice of a friend who suggested complete calm and a diet of just grapes. She cared for him so deeply that she too only ate grapes. This way there would be no temptation to consume anything else. There was not even coffee or tea to drink, at which point I gave her the rest of my cigarettes. I wondered how would she ever get this man's body out of this isolated place on her own, when he dies.

Youngsters catching Eel in the Elands River.

This stunningly beautiful, caring women made a huge impact on me and for years after my encounter, I found myself thinking of her and wondering what had become her.

Years later, at a Farm day in the Elands River Valley, I was approached by a chubby man, who greeted me as if he knew me. I didn't know him at all until he said "I am not sure if you remember me, but we have met before, in the mountains. I have been cured of my incurable illness."

My heart skipped a beat. His beautiful wife could not be far and I so wanted to see her.

I casually asked: "So where is your wife?"

His answer: "Oh, I divorced that old thing, long ago."

6. The Jew and the Marbles.

A Danie Ferreira story translated and retold by Cindy Oberholzer

Rose Cottage, is one of the oldest houses in the street. Some of the locals at the time were The Badenhorsts, Uncle Fred Whitehead and foreman Palmer.

And the Ofsowitz's. Jews who owned the small shop. The Ofsowitz's family become well known amongst the community and surrounds. In Uitenhage, there was Dr Sollie Ofsowitz, a doctor and jewellery shop owner and Mike Ofsowitz, who owned the garage. Close to us was Oldman Lewies Ofsowitz, the small shop owner.

As children we loved Oldman Lewies Ofsowitz, he was spectacular at marbles and we loved playing against him.
We would buy the marbles from him, which were kept in a large glass bottle on the counter. He would then play against us, ultimately resulting in him playing the marbles back into the glass bottle.

7. The Rose and Shamrock.

A Danie Ferreira poem translated and retold by Cindy Oberholzer

John Strydom is married to the lovely Joyce
We rarely get to hear her voice
A wide awake, intelligent, strong women.
But what does she say about her husband's sin?

She says she can prove it's not fair
His mischievous streaks give her grey hair
She sees him, chilling in the field
Shaving biltong, counting his yield.

Then off he goes to shoot a rabbit
And makes a turn past Oom Piet, like a bad habit
She watches him close, to see he does not mock
At which point he's been long sitting at the Rose and Shamrock.

8. The Hero of Delville Wood – Lukas Gouws.

A Danie Ferreira story translated and retold by Cindy Oberholzer

My first encounter with Lukas Gouws was at Tip Tree, where I attended school. He was a tall, lanky chap, tanned dark brown from the sun, with blue eyes. He was easy to chat to and eagerly told stories of being a soldier in the First World War.

"Coincidentally", I fell so ill I could not attend school and had to stay at my grandmother's for a night or two. What do you know, only to share the spare room with Lukas. It was there that he regaled the tragic events of Delville Wood and showed me his scars from where he was shot. A bullet entered the top of his thigh and exited out of the other thigh. He was one of the miracles that survived the onslaught of Delville Wood. "A Hero".

The price for being a survivor, a hero, meant he had to deal with shellshock. With the result that he, by choice, lived an isolated hermit lifestyle, deep in the mountains.

His humble home bordered on a few farms, where he let his sheep and cows graze at will. Once a month he would come down from the mountains on his horse and was accompanied by his red eyed, white bull terrier.

He would visit with the locals, coincidentally, around meal times. This way he could get a few good, hearty meals in.

Once a year, on the day of the annual NG Kerk bazaar, without fail Lukas would attend. This was his day to eat heartily and pack his bags with tasty sweet treats, before heading back to isolation.

This was his life pattern for years.

Until the day of the 'big freeze'. The mountains had frozen over. Lukas did not come down for his routine visit. Some of the local shepherds made a turn at Lukas' house. The door was half open and inside the kitchen lay Lukas Gouws, on his back, dead. The bull terrier, laying over his body, still with the lead around its neck and the other end around Lukas's wrist.

The shepherds could not get anywhere near the body as the dog was wild and wanted to attack. The ever faithful dog lay in watch over his masters body, for what was at least 14 days.

Lukas Gouws's house.

The dog had to be shot, as no one could get near the body. It was only then discovered how the dog managed to stay alive. He had eaten the lower abdomen, the tops and inside of poor Lukas's legs. Strangely the intestines were untouched. So this is how, Lukas Gouws, the hero of Delville Wood, met his end. Thanks to his dog Lukas's secret he had carried for all the years was still intact. You see that day in my grandmother's spare room he showed me how the bullet entered the top of his thigh, removed all his genitals and excited out the other thigh.

Below Bushman rock art, on Luka's farm. Photo taken by the Dodd family, while hiking.

Ds. Fullard, Oom Matie Scheepers and Oom Paul Heyns wrapped him is his threadbare coat and buried him in a shallow, lonely, icy grave next to his beloved dog, deep in the mountains. A Hero's funeral?

9. Did you know?

A Danie Ferreira story translated and retold by Cindy Oberholzer

1893 – Only two English schools were in Uitenhage at that time. Muir College and Riebeeck College. Most children were considered lucky to reach standard six.

10. Drought.

A Danie Ferreira poem translated and retold by Cindy Oberholzer

But no... He wants to expand
He buys a farm in our valley's land
With this move he shows me and you
That our land does have a value.

The die hard who are still here to fight
Cling to the bottom with all their might
We plant our corn without guarantee
And hope for a better year, you see.

A drought farm he did acquire
Dry Kloof was its name not its desire
His first eyesight from his beginners eye
To see the grain dehydrate under the sky.
Clouds rumble, which no one believes
Beneath lay the bone dry leaves
His farm looks like a vast desert
As the last patch of green dies, it hurts.

The wondering birds patrol for a green pool
Resort to hiding in sparse green grass cool
Long last have the prophets of doom foretold
Wherever he casts his eye, doom will unfold.

He constantly comes across as a brick wall
It mulls in him to realize he is so small
Then before him appears a dream so real
The Dry Kloof becomes a watery sea, to once again heal.

11. The "Gullible" Eavesdropper.

A Danie Ferreira story translated and retold by Cindy Oberholzer

The telephone rings, a short and a long or two shorts and two longs or three shorts and a long. Everyone could hear the ring and knew exactly for whom the call was and with this the nosey parkers came running to listen in. The phone made a clink sound and one could guess who the eavesdropper was. Oom Heyns had emphysema, his chest whistled and he always forgot to cover the mouth piece with his hand.

The more people who eavesdropped the weaker the line became. To the point where on one occasion Tant Maria, the eavesdropper, interrupted by blurting out: "Speak up I can't hear" At which point I said "Surely the Holy Satan knows what becomes of those who listen in on conversations."

Auntie Grite was a regular eavedropper. One day the wind blew so hard, I phoned Lourens Snyman to chat about the wind, when I heard a click noise.

I said Loures: "I heard the wind blew so hard in Port Elizabeth, that it blew the Campanile over."

"No, that can't be true." Auntie Grite blurted out: "When did that happen?"

12. Did you know?

A Danie Ferreira story translated and retold by Cindy Oberholzer

1836: There was a grasshopper plague, in the district, which resulted in extreme devastation. The farmers were at their wits end as every conceivable solution to kill them, failed. Deep furrows were dug and canvases were erected alongside them. The farmers 'herded' the grasshoppers into the canvases where they dropped into the furrows and covered with sand. The end result, all the crops were completely destroyed.

13. Ivan's Story.

A Danie Ferreira poem translated and retold by Cindy Oberholzer

Never could one a farmer fault
As Ivan, my neighbour, who never did halt
His heart is large and has no limits
His hand always open to house, church and giving it.

His children he teaches from the Good Book
And along his path you could look
Not a lazy hair on his head
Nor an arrogant air is to be said.

And so life storms around him spin
Perhaps too fast for him to win
Marika unflustered stands next to him
Through thick and thin like a concrete limb.

His mind as sharp as a blade
His story one of a great life made
In his house thousands of safes around
As outside ostriches abound.

Like salt and pepper here and there
His trucks run constantly with total care
Lorries like trains, as no need to skim
Even bigger loads all for him.

He delivers as far as Gauteng
Potatoes large and small on offering
The local co-op buys his corn
Ostriches on their way to Oudtshoorn.

The Citrus house pack his oranges high
And Barclays house, they pack his millions without a lie
The bank assesses his financial strength
To build on and on to his breadth and length.

14. Try Remembering This!

A Danie Ferreira story translated and retold by Cindy Oberholzer

Linear Measurements:

12 inches = 1 foot
3 feet = 1 yard – ahh this is easy you may say, but
5 ½ yards = 1 pole
4 poles = 1 chain
10 chains = 1 furlong
8 furlong = 1 mile
3 miles = 1 league
4 inches = 1 hand
9 inches = 1 span
30 ½ yards = 1 vk pole
40 vk poles = 1 road

Cubic Measurements:

2 pints = 1 quart
4 quarts = 1 gallon
5 ounce = 1 gill
4 gills = 1 pint
2 gallons = 1 peek
4 peeks = 1 bushel
1 bag = 200 lbs

Sundry Measurements:

16 ounce = 1 pound (lbs)
1 stone = 14 pound (lbs)
1 rime = 20 books
1 book = 24 pages.

Without the four gallon tin and an empty whiskey bottle one could not farm. The general diluting table went like this:

1 in 100 =
1 whiskey bottle in 4 paraffin tins
2 tablespoons in 1 whiskey bottle
1 tablespoon = in half a fluid ounce or 4 coins
This is 2 times as big as a desert spoon.
This is 4 times as big as a teaspoon.

But the best of all is the 4 gallon paraffin tin.
A full tin equals the following:
10 lbs bran
20 lbs oats
25 lbs barley
28 lbs mealies
28 lbs potatoes
30 lbs corn, peas or beans
40 lbs coarse salt

Lest we do not forget the money system. £ (pond), s (schilling), d (penny), ½ d (penny), ¼ d (penny) and the Guinea was 21/- (21 schillings).

And at school we had to times, divide, subtract and add these together!

And to think these little ones had to remember all of this.

15. My Worldly Possessions.

A Danie Ferreira story translated and retold by Cindy Oberholzer

1814: at the death of Thomas Ferreira his possessions were listed as:

* 1 male slave * 1 female slave * 2 female children slaves * 3 teenage female slaves * 11 hottentot men * 946 sheep * 18 mules * 2 borrowed roof sheets.

1854: at the death of Soloman Ferreira, in the house at Mistkraal, (Thomas's son) his possessions were listed as:

* 100 sheep and goats * 3 riding horses * 9 breeding horses * 1 span oxen * 1 wagon * 20 cows and calves * half of Erasmuskraal and Miskraal.

He was considered "a man in comfortable circumstances."

16. Did you know?

A Danie Ferreira story translated and retold by Cindy Oberholzer

1875: After the subdivision of the farm Slangenhoekfontein (Tip Tree), a dispute arose between the widow Rosina Elizabeth Vermaak and Agnes Isobella Palmer. The case was taken on appeal and the judgement was delivered by Lord CJ de Villiers, chief justice in the leading case of Vermaak versus Palmer.

In 1975: Exactly 100 years later, history repeated itself. In the case of Ferreira versus Ferreira over the same water rights on the same piece of land.

17. Reaction from Our Farmers.

A Danie Ferreira poem translated and retold by Cindy Oberholzer
P.S. Danie had two nicknames - "Kojak" and more commonly used "Koekoe".

He assembles his tractors without a moan
When before you know it, we hear the drone
From sunrise to sunset without hesitation
And this is all in our deliberation.

Have you heard what Ivan is up to
For this should have nothing to do with me or you
We hear he wants to lead the water some
We not too sure from when's it will come.

He is mad as hell and has lost his marbles
If done too late all he hears is alarm bells
Build a dam with all this doubt
For more than thirteen years of drought.

With all our prayers and all our hope
No water has run down that slope
Let him build a dam with his dough
I think he has forgotten about Sakkie Louw.

Who's dams first gets the water all day
"Oh dear" says Kojak "Oh by the way"
His generous order is way too tall
As the catchment area is way too small.

The rain is too little the dam is too big
If it ever does fill, oh blow me over and call me a pig.

18. The Brother-In-Law and The Whippet.

A Danie Ferreira story translated and retold by Cindy Oberholzer

In and around 1910 the first motor cars arrived in the Elands River. The Model T Ford made its first appearance. Thereafter a variety of other models. The Whippet and the Hubmobile. The trucks were the Thorney Crofts and the British Cammers. Uncle William Snyman had a Napier and Uncle James a Graham motorcar.

In the early years bankruptcy's were unheard of till about 1929, when a few farmers in the region hit a slump. Uncle Natie Ferreira, owner of good lands, The Fonteine, Goosen and Rietgat, he was an excellent farmer but was hit by this slump and became bankrupt.
Everyone was concerned for him and at the auction tried to buy his land and animals back for him. He had a brand new, beautiful, in mint condition Whippet. His brother-in-law suggested that he buys the Whippet and later would sell it back to Natie. The bid fell at - £2 10/-.

"No", said his brother-in-law, "before I return it I would like to service it".
Natie never drove his car again.

19. 1799 – 1812.

A Danie Ferreira story translated and retold by Cindy Oberholzer

The farming community was heavily hit by the intense drought and grasshoppers. This natural disaster stretched as far as the Gamtoos River. The Fish River was the barrier between the Pioneers moving along the Southern Coast and the Tribes folk moving down the East coast. The farmers were instructed to register their Hotentot maids. Dr van der Kemp from the London contingency was instructed to establish a base station at Swartkops River.

Hottentot troops, under the leadership of Stuurman Trompettey and Boesak, moved in and around the area. Murder, theft and manslaughter were the order of the day. The Boere Commandant, Tjaart van der Walt, in 1802, was instructed to fight back against the intruders. Van der Walt rose to the challenge.

1812: Today, Sir John Cradock, issued a proclamation that all Hottentot children between the ages of 8 to 18 years old, who lived on the premises, be registered by the farmers. The farmers were instructed to train all children, from as young as possible, in a farming skill. All Hottentot's were protected against unscrupulous employees.

20. The First Blacks in the Valley.

A Danie Ferreira story translated and retold by Cindy Oberholzer

1857: This was the time of the devastating famine. Around 68 000 black people, out of a group of 105 000, died of hunger. Thousands of starving blacks streamed into the Elands River Valley looking for work and help. They were known as "The thin blacks". Due to their situation they were 'allowed' to stay and hence become the first black people to 'settle' in the area.

Old Dagen, became my Great Grandfathers right hand man. He had two sons, Natie and Peturs. Malgas was their friend. They were really decent people.
There was a time when the Elands River became a "one colour race". First were the Bushman then the Hottentots (Old Faans and Gert Tietes with their families) and then later there was the Matabeles, from Rhodesia, who worked for Uncle Salmantjie.

21. The Love Story.

A Danie Ferreira story translated and retold by Cindy Oberholzer

The love story of the Rudman's and the little Rudmantjies. She who was the mother, slaved to keep the pot on the boil. He who was the father, played with the children under the tree.
The Landstem magazine ran a competition for the loveliest love story. She won first prize. Her 10 children were the proof of her love story.

22. Reminiscing.

A Danie Ferreira poem translated and retold by Cindy Oberholzer

In the meantime twenty years have passed
Just like a dream and in seconds fast
You'll still find some oldies in their home space
While others are resting in a more permanent place.

The road was long and often steep
The disheartening sadness, one never defeats
The tears run down, as you face the winter wind
In the end a rejoicing joy for all who have sinned.

We can look back and hold on steady-ing
To the good, the love and the weddy-ing
The wonder of reminiscing
From sun shines and blessings.

Mystery, hope, the dead a fright
Till when we see again the light
But tonight we feed our dreams
Our 'whenever' hangs over the darkened streams.

Are we glad and will we get
As the great universe may forget
Over unmeasurable abundancy's
Forms part of our rejoiceingly.

Will we know where our loved ones rest
On star dust or as lights guest
A wave of relief flows over our souls
As a light from paradise us boldly holds.

Whitehead family – picking apples.

23. The Money Lender.

A Danie Ferreira story translated and retold by Cindy Oberholzer

Uncle Pietman Rautenbach from the farm Ruefordt, his three daughters, his well brought up wife and his once a year trip to town. The long uphill. Money was scarce. It was the depression years.

He was in great need of £50. He made a loan of £50 from a well-known local, his neighbour, Mr. Henry "Boetie" Gamble, son of Minister Thomas Gamble. He signs his farm as collateral.

When he was ready to pay the £50 back, this turned out to be in vane as he had in fact signed the farm over. The agreement turned out to be an offer to purchase - not a loan.

Everyone tried to help him, lawyers, family and friends. To no avail. The money lender laid claim to the farm and Mr. Pietman Rautenbach lost it all.

Then comes the beautiful letter, written in perfect English, by his wife Mrs. Rautenbach. "Please I know you are a child of God, here is your £50. Let us have the document back."

In the end, Mr. Henry Gamble gave them the right to live on the farm, on condition that they received no visitors, could not cut wood, could not reap any honey, could not hunt, could not trap birds and lest of all could not speak to the workers.

As for Mr. Henry Gamble, after his father's death, he became the minister and held services at the Rose Lane Church.

24. Did You Know?

A Danie Ferreira story translated and retold by Cindy Oberholzer

1804-1813: The Elands River was teaming with game – Zebra's, Kwagga's, Hippopotamus (which were commonly called Sea Cows) and Eland. The game was so heavily hunted that the authorities later had to curtail all hunting activities.

The net result is that the 'vermin' became prolific and the authorities made money available to wipe out the 'vermin'.

For example

Leopard - £ 1,17,6

Jackal and Wolves - £ 1,10,0

Wild cats and Links - 1s/6d

Mongoose and Hawk - 9d.

Leopard skin.

25. But now That Faithful.

A Danie Ferreira poem translated and retold by Cindy Oberholzer

But now that faithful friend has reached the end - of her years
No more does she answer to my calling tears
Her bridle hangs on the wall
Her saddle in her lonely store.

But now that faithful friend has reached the end - of the hoe
She's gone to where all good ponies go
Her voice still echoes in my ears
Her faded blanket after so many years.

But now my faithful friend has reached the end-of my dreams
She's gone like liquid down the streams
My love for her does never part
As her song still echoes in my heart.

George Whitehead Senior and his trusty Horse.

26. Party Lines.

A Danie Ferreira story translated and retold by Cindy Oberholzer

The Telephone: The centre was in Uitenhage and the end of the line was at Tip Tree and much later at Bergplass.
'Old' Lizzie, a black lady, manned the switchboard at Tip Tree. Everyone chatted simultaneouly. My father, Uncle Sanbok, Uncle Heyns and Uncle Noel Whitehead all together.

The cost:
A tiekie to Uitenhage.
6d to Patensie
6d plus a tiekie to Port Elizabeth.
This was all for a three minute connection.

Things were looking up for the Elands River Valley. The bus service ran twice a week and a telephone line for almost every farm.

Uncle Tinus and Uncle Gert Scheepers from Melkhoutboom were full of mischief and from listening in, heard that Aunty Miennie was waiting for her false teeth, which she had ordered. They then found a set of meercat teeth, placed them neatly in a package and address the package to Aunty Miennie. They gave the package to the bus driver, with instructions to deliver it to Aunty Miennie at Weltevrede.

That night they phone Uncle Gert and said: "We believe that Aunty Miennie's teeth arrived with the bus driver today and would like to know how they fit?"

At this point I will rather not deliver any further comment on this incident.

27. Did you know?

A Danie Ferreira story translated and retold by Cindy Oberholzer

1854: There were vegetable fields, vineyards and citrus orchards planted. I can remember that almost every farm in the district had a grape pergola and a vineyard. The book "Uitenhage Past and Present", writes about wine and brandy being brewed. Wool and Afrikaner sheep were farmed as well as Afrikaner cows.

Orchards and ploughed fields.

28. Building of a Dam.

A Danie Ferreira poem translated and retold by Cindy Oberholzer

On expertise a decision was made
Cautiously the blueprint is laid
A final discussion on the dam's wall agreed
The studies done by Mr. DeWet du Preez.

The Engineer's name is John
And advice comes from Ivan, some
For many months much is ridden in and flows
From where these men got it no one knows.

A View over the Elands River.

Day in. Day out. The dust swirls all around
The dam scrappers growl and dust abounds
Getting stuck in the wet pot clay
Chains break and the ground gives way.

Higher and higher climb the tractors
Deeper and deeper sink the contractors
Higher and Higher. Deeper and Deeper
Deeper still, says the Engineer as it gets steeper.

Week on week. Month on month
From before dawn to after dark, it non- stop runnith
The summer sun scorches till men are unrecognised by kin
The winter wind relentlessly peels away their skin.

Tant Mynie has made a hearty meal
And Faan brings the coffee for the meal
On occasions there is boere rusks
Yet another day passes till after dusk.

29. Flood.

A Danie Ferreira poem translated and retold by Cindy Oberholzer

The dam just finished, the rains turn the dust to mud
And on this rain's tail is an enormous flood
The greatest flood was 40 days says Tant Mynie
These rains give this record a run for its money.

Shuddering, rumbling, boiling, frothing
Waves of undulating storm comes a foaming
Thunderous attacks tear over the wall
Relentless rain falls meters tall.
There's nothing that can holt this onslaught
Sweat and anxiety laid in every thought
Water masses move with strength
Another night lays ahead at length.

Then reality dawns on us so free
The bone dry valley a watery sea
History is here and making our places
The farms will turn into glorious oasis's.

Now before us lay fields to be irrigated
Where power and pumps have long awaited
For Ivan, Henry and the Engineer much needed
We show our respect as you have succeeded.

A magnanimous dam is now proudly by our side
With pivots which catapult out our daily pride.

The Elands River in Flood.

30. Sweet Little Lettie.

A Danie Ferreira story translated and retold by Cindy Oberholzer

Total poverty spread over the valley during the depression years.

Many who once owned their farms became squatters on them. It was a common sight to see barefoot white children, barely clothed, cold and starving making their way to school.

On my father's farm, Tip Tree, four or five such families lived as refugees.

Let me take a moment to tell you about these children.

At Highwaters, when it was still a part of Die Fonteine, lived a refugee family, the Claasens. The children went to school with me at Die Fonteine, they were extremely poor and dressed in rags.

The "caring" Miss. Vermaak was our teacher. She bought my sisters old clothes from my mother and gave them to the youngest Claasen child, Little Lettie. She was only allowed to wear the clothes during school times. Her old clothes remained in the teacher's room until home time, when she had to put her old clothes on again.

One day, she could not find her old clothes, as the maid moved them while cleaning the teacher's room. Little Lettie then proceeded to walk across the playground to tell the teacher she could not find her clothes.

Needless to say Little Lettie was buck naked.

The "caring" Miss. Vermaak, in full view of all of us, continuously gave naked Little Lettie a hiding, until she peed herself.

31. Did you know?

A Danie Ferreira story translated and retold by Cindy Oberholzer

The idea to begin a new school for the poverty stricken children of Uitenhage and surrounding areas, was that of Dominie D.J. Pienaar. He took it upon himself to raise money wherever he could. A sum of £ 560 was collected. A piece of ground with a few buildings on it was purchased for £ 700 and a school was opened. The subjects offered were cabinet making, tailoring, blacksmithing, wagon building, shoemaking and farrier. This was the start of the "Poor School" and look at it today. It is the dynamic Danial Pienaar Technical High School.

Ds. Pienaar – in service from 1887 tot 1926.

Ds. Pienaar, Uitenhage thanks you.

32. The "Hellsa" Long Poem.

A Danie Ferreira poem translated and retold by Cindy Oberholzer

At Middlewater farms Skamier
He does his thing without a fear
With pleasure go look at all he tries
What you see will be a surprise.

The Americans taught him all
From shearing sheep to planting clover tall
Us neighbours were left dumbstruck
The old ways now don't have to rely on luck.

Our farming was all cattle specific
From now on we will be all scientific
Then the pests will not tease and bolt
The plagues will gratefully come to a halt.

As the drought shows its vicious teeth
Skamier shows us waterways to quench the heat
You see he learned how to irrigate
With limited resources that do not forsake.

***

And before the organ in the church
Ada sits, in her pretty skirt, sits on her perch
It's here that she swings her sceptre
She swings it high and low spreading the protector.

As Sydney does as he pleases
In each hand a nine mill he teases
It's as if he wants to wage a war
Lizelle will have to soften him a whole lot more.
Her budget is always being tested
As at Rocklands it has now manifested
It hits her like a lightning bolt
She must still pay for the peaches and salt.

***

Here races Matie with commotion amplified
His bakkie has now been pimped and modified
Sporting two new exhausts and all
Now he rides in style with head held tall.

For goodness sake, the road is not a race track
Alta is now angry and giving all flack
From now on she professes
She will be driving she confesses

She hears a loud commotion, what could she do
At Afdak cars just miss each other, but who
As Elno has the sharp turn to guestimate
Then closes his eyes and hopes his bowels do not forsake.

***

It was as such, at that present
The unharnessed were now blessed with pleasant
Naartjies here and Peaches there
And Avos if there were to spare.

Everyone loads up delicious fruit
Little few ever pay the loot
There was one in particular who flous
He came along with chocolates to smous.

The men farm the pigs all too fat
The ladies make kooksisters by the vat
Everyone gets ready for the church bazaar
A success no doubt everyone will declare thus far.

***

His short steel pipe and Boxer tobacco
His hard match sticks on the shelf just so
His beautiful wife and his stylish moustache
Our black police man who shows such class.

One always finds him awake and alert
Always at the ready to protect all against hurt
In time of need to our right hand we revert
Just a small note I'd like to add, also a pumpkin expert.

***

We are living through dark times
So finds Willem as his story unwinds
His truck breaks down in Jeffrey's Bay
But a kind soul did not leave him in the fray.

However his corn was still on the truck
His dogs and birds were with it stuck
He returns in a flash to get up and going
Sadly to return too late as the evil had been on the taking.

He chomps and tears with a bitter liver
And swears them from here to the Kei River
He says to Rinda, it's goodbye
The truck and goods are long gone to the Transkei.

***

On occasions, with great excitement
A social, for all is organised and invited
Oh and how Stefaan's taps the floor
He rocks and rolls with all the ladies who adore.

You see he had lessons in the Bay
About Dirty Dancing and how they sway
He is now considered smoking hot
By all the girls as he is now hot to trot.

***

Chummy's belief is so strong
He is a lamb of God for many a year's long
He reads the book from morning till night
And boy he can talk about serving in God's light.

The drought that lingers for years on end
Rests heavily on ones nerves, no longer can one pretend
We must caution ourselves to not erupt
If all the farmers become bankrupt.

He goois a dop, a shot to hit the spot
His worries shoot his blood pressure up, a lot.
Where is Alwin quick phone Kraai
Sends old Tobie to look, with a sigh.

Then Marie lays the table with all she is making
With sweet potatoes, rice and bacon
She thinks her boyfriend will stay and eat
But instead his off to his booked rugby seat.

Curiously everyone checks what Danie is up to
Oh my word, the Kojak is kissing who and who
Cecile greets everyone with a hearty laugh
Her garden is booming and is a perfected craft.

***

She pours herself a glass full not low
As we know she is fond of her Gin just so
She loves her fashion and stylish outfits
And gladly wears her pants with a nice tight fit.

Her minis are break neckingly pure sin
She looks just like a mannequin
When Ronnie decides to holiday
Ewald offers to stand in without dismay.

He's off to feed their dogs eagerly
But they corner him so and have him pressingly
His body broke like a reed
Eventually they left him at his heed.

Their blood ran red through their eyes
They growled and gnawed at his demise
He prayed like Daniël in the lion's den a shivering
When he saw their jaws watering.

Oubaas's dogs please please sit
As I have now in my pants did shit
Oh Marlene is running to help poor Ewald
As Ronnie is still shouting orders with a jolt.

***

His here, his there, his hot and stout
This goes on year in, year out
He says he is coaching tennis in a flap
But Marlene thinks he's speaking crap.

As people have seen him out and around
Riding is his car as they have frowned
They think he is a smooth operator so they flook
Just like the President, he does look.

***

At Cotswold Little Louis is building a dam
It's shearing season and the sheep are with lamb
The orphan lambs are performing so that he cannot think
While the Rooikat is eyeing into what his teeth can sink.

The pump dies and the sprayer stops
He kicks it so that it makes him hop
He grabs the CB spluttering and fuming
Come in Erika, come in, come in.

Quickly an assessment is made in kind
By Mamma Fier as she's of sound mind
Calmly she feeds the lambs their milk
And sprays the veggies so they don't wilt.

She sorts the shorn wool, without a hiss
As something there seems to be amiss
Now the cows are out and he wants to shout
Oh my word poor old Louis stands stout.

He realises it's too late hence
He scrums the cows back through the fence
At which point he is now wide awake, oh my
As it felt as if he just scored a try.

Big Boy rises in the early morn it's said
Then slides his comb over his balding head
He watches and loves his fowls without a doubt
As Swartkop feeds and then lets them out.

Her daily chores are drawing to a close
As he calls to her" "Are the chickens in, vrou?"
His started learning Dutch, to treasure
Then pours a cognac on the measure .

We think the world revolves around our fuss
But it does not stand on attention for us
This she says and so it seems to me
My possessions are speaking, to me, so free.

He walks a ways down the path, so worn
Till behind the old plank shed and onto the lawn
He is looking for an old grain bag
For to cover his wife's head, as for sure she's gone mad.

***

And as for the Black Politics, on and on
Is our Big Boy sick to death of this con
The government is like a coffee can
Which stands up for the Black man.

The coffee has been poured, it's true
As Mandela has played this trough
The HKGK is still our friend
As it stand for us at Kodesa to mend.

***

With all due respect his going to take a leap
As he believes in his cattle and his sheep
Down to his marrow bones is John a boer, I say
As a quick brandy shot and then it's work all day.

He could drive his bakkie with far more care
However he's on the hunt for a bushbuck ram not mare
He revs and rides the bakkie all out
And shoots the buck till he has a heap so stout.

You can hear him coming from a mile away
As over the intercom he shouts loudly his say
Hel-lo there, to the all who have sinned
His lips go flapping in the wind.

The day goes on at the river pan
Where is De Witt, Fanie and Stan
They promised us they would come even if hot
And meet us at the watering spot.

***

With mother around the farm all day
Does butter melt in all that her son says
He leads her around the bush you see
Then when she's away he parties heartily and irresponsibly.

He drinks all the Coke and eats all the cheese
While the cats away the mouse is at ease
His LV he says he can prove if he may
While his mischief makes his mother grey.

She sees him in the field which is so wrong
As he is lazing, loafing and singing a song
Then off he is to shoot some crows
But ends up at Piet and no one knows.

She makes a turn to catch him at Piet
But he's long left there, with all his kit
You see he's been sitting at the Rose.
For how long, nobody knows.

Productive is Joyce, his wife
She cooks, cleans and pays without strife
She runs the books to the last cent
And knows all the tricks which SARS meant.

The rands and cents are clear to her
The receiver will never notice the odd slur
If here or there a Rand is in a 'trance'
As her books are always in balance.

Bloublits sings with great delight
He pours himself another for the night
He is a stock car racer and number one
He crashes all cars, under the sun.

For Oumies is the sport so great
So she decides to test her fate
She broadsides this way and that
And lands herself in a ditch, that's that.

***

Someone caused a hell of a delay
At Stilgenoeg, was Tommy Doyle now in dismay
As someone locked the gate so dim
Now sit and wait, is what is in stall for him.

By all his neighbours he was loved
Until one day he was handcuffed
His dogs were shot, his best friend dead
"Sy moer" was all that Sylvy said.

I ponder on my worthiness
As I think on how she lives alone, in her simpleness
To blame is not her story
And never seeks her deserved glory.

Who finds no fault, I am told
She has a heart of pure gold
Dear Monica know this to be true
We will never, yes never, forget you.

***

For years and years in this old building
Did Mrs. Richbiter instruct us in our schooling
The mothers and fathers she did teach
Till later on their children's, children she did reach.

She taught us our ABC's
The dog does bark and the cat climbs trees
To Lena Richbiter we say thanks a lot
You laid a corner stone, in this here spot.

Great respect did Ian have
When Jenny smacked the kids till sad
Little Conrad screamed so desperately
While Shaun yells out, my bum's on fire so suddenly.

The girls all took their leave in pain
And stood outside in the rain
That's when Mr. Delport had to decide
The little school will now close with pride.

Our little school which stood for years
We will not forget, say the pupils in tears.
Your end has come so suddenly
Jan, Sannie and Oom Freek, we thank you enduringly.

For more than one hundred years you did last
Through your threshold we did pass
You had our steadfast future in your sight
Our guiding arrow through the night.

I, once again with my broken heart
Say Goodbye to our Jenny, before I depart.

33. Have you ever seen the Cape?

A Danie Ferreira story translated and retold by Cindy Oberholzer

At break time we would play outside. We made up a new game were we would ask: "Have you seen the Cape at all?" If you said no. You would be turned upside down and swung around by your feet.

I asked Rientjie, a little white haired girl, in Sub A: "Have you seen the Cape at all?" She said no, she had not. So I turned her upside down and swung her round and round by her feet. Her dress slide up over her head.

Only to realize that the dress is all she had on!

34. Never Forget From Where You've Come.

A Danie Ferreira story translated and retold by Cindy Oberholzer

Sol Marais, a young uneducated child lived with his parents on the farm Pereboom. His father worked for Danie Marais, the owner. The year was 1920.
Sol would have to chop wood to assist his parents eke out a living. With a miss-matched team of cows and oxen he would transport his wood to the market for which he would receive a few shielings.

Even though he could not go to school. On the farm he built a post office, a shop, a butcher and a pound. He also built a school. The first teacher was a Mr. Van Lingen. The farm was bought with a bond and when times got tough, the family were retrenched.

The family left the farm and Sol went his own way. He got a small job which paid £ 1 10 per month. At night he was completely alone, still a child, in a wagon.

Pereboom School built by Sol Marais.

One Saturday in 1930, Sol found himself on the Uitenhage station with £ 3 in his pocket and a suitcase in hand waiting for a train. He was heading for the gold mines on the Rand, 700 miles away from his birthplace.

Fortunately he did not know how difficult it would be, as an outsider, to get work. As all jobs asked for schooled applicants.

After days of fruitless job hunting, going from house to house. For the first time in his life he began to panic and his self-worth was shattered. He tried to shake off this feeling however it had taken its hold. His stomach had been empty for days when he decided to make his way back to Uitenhage, back home to the Elands River. When out of the blue he received a small job, to help plaster a house. He was thrilled to have this job no matter how small, as it led to house maintenance work, washing and polishing cars, furniture repairs, plastering, wallpapering, floor sanding and polishing for hotels and houses. All this just for board and lodging.

His luck turned after 6 months when he got work on a mine in Johannesburg. They allowed him to enrol into the mine school. He is now a mine worker at 3 shielings and 9 pennies per day. After 15 months he completed his course and achieved a General Mineworkers Certificate, with honours.

He now reports for duty at the Crown Mines at £ 50 per month. He became much admired and liked by his co-workers.

One day the head of the mines called him into his office. To his absolute joy and shock he was promoted to Instructor of the mine school. Sol was slowly climbing the ladder. He never looked back. From here on out he was offered better and better jobs.

He received a post as manager of the Nama Line Works – Namaqualand and leaves the City of Gold for good. In this world Sol becomes a pioneer. Ultimately becoming the owner of the biggest farm land and cattle farm in South West Africa.

After the death of his wife, Sol decided to return to the Elands River, to show his new wife where he grew up. His new wife was none other than Hope van Lingen, daughter of Mr. van Lingen, the first teacher of the school at – Pereboom.
The school he built with his own two child hands.

(Sol died 2009 just before his 98th birthday.)

35. Did you Know?

A Danie Ferreira story translated and retold by Cindy Oberholzer

The mode of transport around 1900 – 1910 was mainly ox wagons, horse carts and donkey wagons. Horses were hard to come by due to the Boer War and with the outbreak of horse flu, horses became extremely scarce.

36. Hard Times – Hard Times.

A Danie Ferreira story translated and retold by Cindy Oberholzer

* The young Alberts, who dressed in clothes made from mealie bags, were always hungry. Fortunately it was prickly pear season. The children grew their thumb nails long, which were used as a knife to peel the skins off the prickly pears. So as to eat the fruit. The 'caring' Miss Vermaak, our teacher, had had enough and in a rage cut off the children's finger nails. Little did she know that this was their only means of eating something on their way to school.

* At The Fonteine one day I witnessed one of the Claasen's daughters, Susan, picking out the mealies from the dogs food, which had been thrown into the half cut out tyre.

* Our reading book from Sub. A to Std. 6 was - Lees met Lus (Read with Desire). The story was beautiful. One day, our teacher, the 'caring' Miss Vermaak read us a story about a black family, their habits and how they slept. We began to laugh wholeheartedly, without a

care. Miss. Vermaak also laughed. She noticed Rientjie sitting quietly. She asked Rientjie: "And what do you sleep on?" "I too sleep on a sack Miss."

* The young Alberts walked down from the hill to school. They passed my father's orchards. They did not pick the figs, however they did pick up the skins from the ground. One of the children went by the nickname Broek. Broek fell very ill at school one day and asked Miss Loubscher to leave the room. She refused him and chased him back to his desk. He could not take it anymore, he turned around and tried to run outside. When he passed her table he threw up.

His breakfast – fig skins and water.

* The depression years stretched on endlessly. These were difficult times, money was scarce and food scarcer. The children would walk along this long Elands River Road asking for food. I can recall the children coming to ask my mother for a piece of bread.

37. Did you Know?

A Danie Ferreira story translated and retold by Cindy Oberholzer

The Rev. Honourable Thomas Gamble, minister at Rose Lane from July 1897. He was also the architect of the historically beautiful little church at Doringhoek, which was built and towered four or five levels against the steep slope.

38. From the Book.

A Danie Ferreira story translated and retold by Cindy Oberholzer

The depression years and the drought brought a new kind of question. The question of the poor White. Money was scarce and food even scarcer.

To relieve this dire situation every attempt to create work opportunities were made by the Hertsog reign.

Farmers who owned their farms could apply to have farm dams built, as long as the dams were approved and the work would be given to the white workers, who were divided into teams. Almost every farm made use of this opportunity.

The work was mostly hard work. The loose ground was carted away by dam scoops powered by two donkeys. The salaries were a meagre one shieling and eight pennies per day.

The poor whites were also used to build and maintain the roads.

Around 1936 to 1938, Old man Tossie Ferreira had a shop at Tip Tree. He supplied these men with food and clothes. Everything on the book. Men by the names of: De Lange, Deysel, Knoetze, McLeod and Greef. The men would say that my grandfather's shop was too expensive. Here is an extract from De Lange's purchases from that book.

De Lange - 4 December 1937:

1 shirt	3/6	(35c)
25 lbs mealie meal	2/6	(25c)
25 lbs bread meal	4/-	(40c)

4 lbs sugar	1/-	(10c)
1 lbs coffee	3d	(2 ½ c)
2 tins sardines	6d	(5c)
1 tin salmon	9d	(7 ½ c)
1 slaughtered ewe	8/-	(80 c)
	--	
	£1 1s 3d total	(R2.05)

What always shocks me is – dam building is like moving mountains and the fuel for this mammoth task is flour, sardines, coffee and occasionally meat.

The hard workers.

Over time the wheel did turn and of these men, who built these dams, came out on top. In later years they got jobs managing the building of such dams.

39. Did you Know?

A Danie Ferreira story translated and retold by Cindy Oberholzer

After 1983 – 13 years of drought followed. The first rains arrived in 1996, and as fate will have it, a flood. This also marked the end of the glory days which the Elands River experienced. It was the end of the production of grain.
"It was the worst of times." Elands River was no longer a grain producing region.

40. A Day at School.

A Danie Ferreira story translated and retold by Cindy Oberholzer

There were no desks for the children. We sat on long benches with no back rests. Four or five children would sit on one bench, with a sort of plank in front of them, which served as a desk. Our teacher had a chair and a desk. We also had a black board with a felt eraser.

Each child was issued with a slate and a slate pencil. We were not allowed to write with a blunt pencil, however we could sharpen the pencil on a stone during break time or after school. In the corner of the classroom was a cloth with which we could wipe our slate clean.

The older children were taught to write in pen and ink. A pot of ink was issued to each of these children. The pen had a loose nib. It was extremely difficult to write with the pen and ink, well you see blotches have no mercy. We used blotting paper and ruined cloths with the ink. Our parents had to help with the blotches as they would assist by putting a little salt and water on the mistake. The salt absorbed most of the ink, however there always remained a spot.

The lessons were difficult, as we were just small children and the mistakes were many. We would have to sit in the corner while we corrected our mistakes, with cloth. It was so much easier to correct it with a little spit and your finger.

It was cold in the mornings and the school was far. We had to walk through the bush and down a valley, hence we got to school sopping wet and frozen. Well this lead to cold season and all the little noses constantly ran. We did not have handkerchiefs so our long sleeve shirts had to do. Our pants never fitted us properly so we wore braces to solve that problem.

41. Did you Know?

A Danie Ferreira story translated and retold by Cindy Oberholzer

The Elands River Road was proclaimed a Divisional Road in the year 1900.

42. Boys will be Boys.

A Danie Ferreira story translated and retold by Cindy Oberholzer

Only the privileged children continued with school after Standard 6. The schools at the time were Muir and Riebeeck College. By the way, in 1913 my father was a prefect at Muir College.

In those years Ds. Pienaar was the minister of the NG Kerk in Uitenhage. He was also the manager of Riebeeck College, which was a church school in 1879. The church had a 50% representation on the managing of Riebeeck, and Ds. Pienaar was at the helm.

Riebeeck's Hostel is a double story building. News went around that the girls hostel was being visited by some young gentlemen from town.

Ds. Pienaar got wind of this and went to investigate the second floor himself. When the signal was given, he lowered the bed sheets, out the window, to the waiting eager gentlemen below.

Huge was his surprise when the first gentlemen helped through the window was in fact his own son.

43. Did you Know?

A Danie Ferreira story translated and retold by Cindy Oberholzer

Ferreira means - yster of hoefsmid. In English – Farrier.

44. All the Little Schools.

A Danie Ferreira story translated and retold by Cindy Oberholzer

In the Elands River many small farm schools were established on the farms themselves. Most of the teachers, both male and female came from overseas.

At Melkhoutboom, owned at the time by Oom Gert Scheepers, the teacher was a Miss. Ilva Stow. She taught from 1890 and was Uncle Heyns and my father's teacher.

Doringhoek was the second school. The teacher was often drunk and fell asleep in the oddest of places. He thought no one knew where he was, however everyone knew where he was, as you see, his faithful horse, Confidence, would always stand and watch over him.

The 'Old' Rose Cottage School

The third school was at Pereboom. It was a long stone building. The school began in 1926 and the first teacher was Mr. WJR van Lingen.

Thereafter schools popped up like mushrooms. At Rose Cottage, The Fonteine, Tip Tree, Afdak, Highwaters and later at Cotswold.

A certain Mr. Daan Dippenaar ran the school at Highwaters. He was one of a quadruplet from Graaff Reinet. Instead of using a cane to discipline the children, on one occasion he dragged Alex Heyns and his sister Rita to the dam and washed their faces with water, as they were sleeping in class. Uncle Paul, Alex's father, got wind of this incident and the "cat was out the bag". He said: "My children have bathed and are clean!"

These were one-man schools. All the children were bundled into one room, the standards where from Sub A to Standard 6. The net result was often comical.

On one occasion the teacher was teaching the Standard 5 children English. The lesson was about 'honde' (dogs) and 'klein hondjies' (puppies). The next day the teacher asked the class what do you call a 'klein hondjie' in English. No one knew, except for one little Sub A, coincidentally that would be me.
"Well, come tell me what is a 'klein hondjie' in English?"
I proudly pushed my chest out and said: "It is a Big Daddy".

Mr. Siddle, the school inspector, would come visit the school once a year. His mode of transport was a horse and cart.

I was elected to read in English in front of Mr. Siddle. The story was from the book Little Chick Lick: "Little Chick Lick swallowed an acorn and he choked in his little throat throat."
"What did Little Chick do?" asked Mr. Siddle.
I answered: "He throat throat in his little choke choke."

The 'New' Rose Cottage School

45. Did you know?

A Danie Ferreira story translated and retold by Cindy Oberholzer

Uitenhage – The old jail in Caledon Street where the BOE Bank is presently, was where prisoners would be caned, in front of everyone. Six strikes with a cane.

Years previously, hangings took place at the same place, for all to see. Later the process became more 'civil' and the hangings were moved to behind the jail, but still within full view, for all.

46. The Donkey.

A Danie Ferreira story translated and retold by Cindy Oberholzer

The donkey was a button. On certain days we could only speak English. If you had the Donkey and you caught one of your friends speaking Afrikaans, you had to give him the Donkey. At the end of the day the one holding the Donkey was punished. Six strikes with the cane. No one knew who had the Donkey and no one knew how to speak English. I often found myself at the end of the day with the Donkey and the cane across my bum.

Rosa Snyman so wanted to be English. She would end her comprehensions and letters : "Your friend. Rosa 'Cutman'."

At break time I found that my sandwiches had gone missing.
I looked and looked and finally said: "Who's got my bread?" Rosa Snyman stormed up to me and gave me the Donkey.
I asked: "Why you give me the Donkey?"

She replied: "'Got' – Is a 'swear' word."
What did I know, this was Rosa 'Cutman', I took the Donkey.

47. The Police.

A Danie Ferreira story translated and retold by Cindy Oberholzer

At the Meadows, Uncle Freddie Whitehead's farm, a police station was established. It was simple – one man on foot.

Crime was almost non existent. Maybe one or two stolen sheep per year. When the culprit was caught he was made to carry the slaughtered sheep and when asked what was his crime. He would have to answer: "I slaughtered a sheep."

Later a police station was established at Tip Tree. The station was also simple. The men, their helmets, their horses, the stables and the constant cleaning of the stables. The police men were Uncle Fred Nel and Uncle Willie Nel.

With time the station was equipped with a motorbike, but still the street remained in peace, with no crime.

A while later the police station became an actual police station. The two-man station was now equipped with a bakkie. Now there was a need to find 'work'.

The policemen did their jobs far too well and the farmers began to became frustrated. On Mondays there was no one at work, as all the staff were in the Tip Tree jail.

This bakkie brought on a time of conflict.

48. The Bench in the Church.

A Danie Ferreira story translated and retold by Cindy Oberholzer

The school at Rose Cottage was an outside room next to a homestead. The teacher at the time was a Mr. Kellerman. Once a month this room was also used to hold a church service.

The 'Old' Rose Cottage School

The benches were placed in rows. Each family sat on the same bench every service. They felt this was their place and would be proud to say they had been sitting there for 5 years or so.

Uncle Gert Marais, from Bergplaas, his wife and their team of children, with a tight squeeze, sat their bench full.

Then the Diphtheria epidemic broke out. We heard the sickness had reached the Marais, and saw the ambulance arrive from town.

However we were shocked to see at the next Rose Cottage church service on the bench sat Uncle Gert and his wife – alone.

One of the old church benches.

49. Everyone is Welcome to the Funeral.

A Danie Ferreira story translated and retold by Cindy Oberholzer

On the day of Uncle Freddie's funeral, under the old Oak Trees, at his farm - The Meadows, a memorable occasion was marked. The minister delivered a moving message, everyone was captured in the moment. At which point the minister turned to the many black attendees, welcomed and thanked them for their attendance.

He started his speech with: "A very big thank you and a special word of gratitude to all Uncle Freddie's staff for attending."

With this, from the mountains came a loud bellowing baboon bark: "Boggom!"

50. Crackshot.

A Danie Ferreira story translated and retold by Cindy Oberholzer

Uncle Freddie's son John was a crackshot. No one – yes – no one could handle a gun better than he.

James Berrington, later the owner of the farm Tip Tree, invited John and myself out to shoot a few Duikers.

When we arrived James said to John: "I want to show you something impressive."

John said: "Yes. Please, I would like to see something nice."
James brought out his gun. A genuine German Mauser: "With this gun" he said "you can make every shot count."

We went into the veld, I had my 303. John had his triple two. When the first buck appeared shots were fired. It fell. "That was my shot." said James. We went to look – headshot. Triple Two, sorry James. The cat was out the bag. John shot seventeen duikers one after the other. James nothing and myself nothing. To crown it all, just for fun John shot a few pheasants, in full flight, out the sky.

One night, a few weeks thereafter, John and I went bushbuck hunting at the Sandriver. I had a permit which allowed us to hunt with a light. We rode to the top of a koppie and shone the torch toward the horizon of the next koppie. There stood a buck. We could only see its eyes shining with the light.

I asked: "What is that?"
He said: "It's a kudu cow, the biggest I've ever seen in my life. Should I shoot it?"
I said: "Shoot!"

John shoots, as the bullet hits, the buck bounces into the air. Crackshot. We got there to discover is was in fact not a Kudu Cow but a small young Grysbok. One shot, to the head.

Hunting and Riding was taught young.

51. The Postman.

A Danie Ferreira story translated and retold by Cindy Oberholzer

Around 1900, Elands River was now on the "map". With the result a post office was established. Once a week, Captain, would run the post from Melkhoutboom to Uitenhage, in one day. He would then sleep in Uitenhage and run back with the post the next day.

As fate would have it. Captain got wind of a certain skellem visiting his wife on the nights he had to stay in Uitenhage.

His next trip he delivered his post in Uitenhage, filled his bag, and ran back home.

Round trip: 140 km !

52. The Mules.

A Danie Ferreira story translated and retold by Cindy Oberholzer

The Mule in the valley need to be acknowledged and recognied for their hard work and sacrifices.

Then along comes the Runderpes. Cattle died by the thousands. Oxen and Dairy Cows started to become scarce. The alternative was the donkeys, horses and mules. Farmers began to breed mules. One could still get female horses from the Free State. Have them covered by a donkey and there you have it - a mule. Not old mangie donkeys but beautiful huge black "Catelonial Jacks" were bred. Every now and then a dunce was born, which reminded one of a human dwalf.

It wasn't difficult to teach them to be cart animals. The mules quickly learned that the word "Hoi" meant stand still. Then the whole team were fitted with their bridles and harnesess.

The roads were difficult especially the turns and hills near the Sand and Bulk Rivers. My uncle and cousin would transport their wool with a mule wagon all the way to Port Elizabeth. On one of the corners, at the top of the Sand River, the driver could not make the tight bend with the team. The rig tumbled down the embankment with the mules, wagon, chains, yolk and wool all crashing down. A tragedy. The mules had broken their legs and had to be shot.

Transport

In 1920 attention was given to the road and a team of labourers under the leadership of Mr. Kleinhans, who lived at the Bulk River, he was issued with two mules and a scotch cart.

53. Did you Know?

A Danie Ferreira story translated and retold by Cindy Oberholzer

Once a year an ox wagon, from Jeffrey's Bay, would pass through selling dried fish. Which was a treat, so far from the sea. We ate fish for months thereafter.

54. The Honeymoon.

A Danie Ferreira story translated and retold by Cindy Oberholzer

Mr. Henry "Boetie" Gamble, son of the Minister Thomas Gamble, was an eccentric person. He was a pupil at Grey College in Port Elizabeth. He had a full dossier, Afrikaans, English and Latin. On the farm and perhaps in town, to protect him from all weather, wind, rain and the cold he wore a grain bag. He would say: "I can dress like a king but I prefer to go like a beggar!"

In the later years of his life he found himself engaged to be married for the first time. As tradition would have it they were to go on honeymoon. He to Cape Town and she to Durban.

55. Hard Times – For the Ants.

A Danie Ferreira story translated and retold by Cindy Oberholzer

Christmas, 1931. The day was swelteringly hot. I will not forget the ants that day. The ground got so hot it began to cook the ants. They had to get out. They literally swarmed and attacked us. My father gave us kettles of hot water and instructed us children to pour the water over the ants.

On old year's day, 1932, the drought broke so that evening there was much jovial partying and dancing, but before the night was over the rains become like a torrent. Dance partners had to move away from each other to avoid the rising waters.

As I think back on the ants they had it tough, thirst, heat stroke, hot water and drowning, all in two weeks.

56. Highlights of Farming.

A Danie Ferreira story translated and retold by Cindy Oberholzer

Doornhoek.

Well known for its apples. Especially one variation – the late bloomers, not regular bloomers, but late. The ground was good and there was plenty of water. The apples were of the best quality. You could smell the aroma of ripe apples miles away from Doornhoek.

The fruits of the family's labour.

The Hoek

The area was progressive and industrious, with a fully functioning water mill. Farmers came from all over with their ox wagons of wheat and corn to be milled. Two water canals supplied The Hoek and Doornhoek with water.

Picking fruit was a family affair.

Then came the twist in the tale. Uncle Neelman Rautenbach, the vowner sells, the Sand River water from The Hoek and Doornhoek to Port Elizabeth municipality, for £ 5 000. There was still enough water in the Elands River to meet Doornhoek and The Hoek's people's needs.

Uncle Neelman is now stinking rich, £ 5 000 is a lot of money. Uncle Neelman builds himself a huge house. He enlisted an artist from London to paint a mural the full length of the stoep wall. He orders an engine and pump from England and pumps the water out of the Elands River, there you have it no problem. Money is full up, water is full up. The trees bring in their money's worth as prices are good.

Then arrives the drought and that is the end of the good era.

57. A Run in with the Law.

A Danie Ferreira story translated and retold by Cindy Oberholzer

Fannie Snyman, from Rose Cottage, was riding around, in her Jeep, without a licence. Basson, the police man, chased her on his bike, she got such a fright she dashed away. She headed towards Goosens driveway with Basson hot on her heels. She sped her way to Rinda Snyman who was living in the stone house. Fannie feel into Rinda's doorway and locked it behind her. As for the police man Basson, he was left out-foxed.

58. The Fire.

A Danie Ferreira story translated and retold by Cindy Oberholzer

To farm with cattle on the grasslands in the Elands River is very difficult. To get fresh grazing for cattle one must first save the land and then burn it. Many of the farms border on Bosbou. The farmers and Bosbou successfully work closely together. However on occasions there are problems.

Permission to burn must first be obtained from the landbou technical division and all the neighbours must be notified of what date the burning will occur.
Sometimes with comical outcomes. Heinrich van Tonder, owner of The Hoek, at the time which, shared its borders with The Island, owned by Mr. Gamble and the Ferreira's on Trisha. They had met with the fire requirements and prepared to burn.

Everyone pitched to start with the burning, except for Mr. Gamble who refused to help, as he felt the day was not right. We phoned technical services and they agree with Mr. Gamble it is not a good day to burn. We are not allowed to burn, it is way too hot and the north wind is blowing too strong.
Heinrich says to me: "Koekoe we are going to burn and if Gamble pitches up, I will donner him myself."

We started the fire ourselves and everything ran smoothly until the fire reached the peak of the mountain when the North wind began to run amok, the flames shot thirty, forty feet into the sky, thundering its way to Loskop.

I heard someone shout out: "Help me." I ran as I thought Heinrich had been trapped in the flames.
Instead I found him in an all too familiar position, kneeling hands together above his head shouting to the sky: "Please Lord God. Help me just for today. If they choose me again to be a Deccan in the church I will accept the position immediately."

59. The Folks of the Elands River's 70's

This was recited at the end of the year Boerevereniging (Farmers Association) function in 1992, at Verkeerdedrif. A Danie Ferreira poem translated and retold by Cindy Oberholzer

At Wide Horizon you'll turn in
This is where our kloof begins
Here no one gets away with anything
Even when there is nothing for which to sing.

Sometimes tears roll, that is our fate
Even when it's way too late
But still our gall continues to spit
So off to church to sing and sit.

Rinda in front, on her throne
Lena clears her throat with a moan
Lucille's now singing a beat ahead.
Jan trudging behind, his notes like lead.
A little primitive, we did not thrive
But after a while a letter did arrive
Announcing that Jan's niece is to visit from the town, so gritty
This would be Johannesburg, the Gold City.

Preparations, Preparations, oh Aunt Hettie crows
And lines everyone up along the wall in a row
We all must be washed squeaky clean, head to toe
To welcome our honoured guest, if you must know.

Oh hell what's happening old Freek
Go wash the red paint from your cheek
And check your long nails, pants and comb
As we are getting a visit from Mr. Sodome.

We celebrate when the wheat harvest is good, as we must
Or bite our lips when along comes the dreaded rust
Oh Lord, here comes the drought and our dismay
The overdrafts and dread, but still we stay.

We sometimes introduce Willem as just plain Will
We found him in Jansenville
He is now our Church Councillor, who follows Gods codes
But mainly, Will fights for a better road.

He, occasionally, does his duty as councillor.
And yes duty does make him familiar.
His duty is done and how he likes to shine
Then grinds his teeth till they are all fine.

His wife is kind, good and in his marriage
She spurs him on and gives him courage
But this is too much for Uncle James
That Rinda is now colluding with the Nattes, so lame.

Wait says Aunt Anne, I have a plan
Put strychnine in the fruit my man
As we all know she's a 'cat'
And in turn may eat the birds, when fat.

Our front doors have never locked
As you see everyone knows who's is who, before they've even stopped
If a car drives on past
We know who driving, even when fast.

Farmers wives are extremely rare
They are few and far between, so take care
No fear she will slaughter a sheep or a duck
Her motto is, my children and I, so with us don't muck.

We both have a lot in common, you see
We will never money lend, we want to stay debt free
Together into old age, we are an enduring pair
This you will witness by our greying hair.

Nephew Lourens is planting his wheat field
However he remains struggling with his yield
His aim is four thousand bags to store in his pit
Ag no, says Sol, that's extremely shit.

Verkeerdedrif you must avoid
This is where calamity reigns and lives destroyed
His name is Coenie believe me it's true
A Sportsman and mean prankster that's him, that's who.

Old friend best warn your wife
A swimming pool built to cool his life
Old Anna Tunis had to toil, build and think
Then ask for mercy to have a break and a drink.

Dead set and determined is Monica dear
Attends to her garden and flowers without fear
But often does not understand
Why her husband moans and groans at her plan.

During "riots" our friends are in dismay
Even Rita is getting worked up on this day
O come what may, Our Father protect us from this fray
Lest our throats be sliced, for nothing, today.

I will never blow my own trumpet
Then I married a women who could nag and huff it
She was brought up in Vensterhoek
O magtie. O heavens can she swear, growl and vloek.

She still stands by me, as through life we sail
And daily fights for us tooth and nail
Even father-in-law slinks off timidly
When she chooses to free her thoughts expressively.

Dear Lucille and Old Jan
Are all that remains from the old group of fun
A better pair you will not find in our constellation
Even though last week they spoke of separation.

So we shout and laugh and jol together
And never will judge our friends, forever
We drink our Lieberstein with utmost ease
And never miss communion and that's not a tease.

A good impression we elude so sincerely
To all who live around us freely
Even George or Lena or even Aunt Fien
Have never seen us drunk or obscene.

Myself, I do not want to miss my land
But know for sure you'll understand
A Jackal's prize is his own tail
And what is mine now worth, so frail.

60. The Aftermath of Burning.

A Danie Ferreira story translated and retold by Cindy Oberholzer

Great tragedy's happened in the past with regards to out of controlled fires.

The fire, which Jannie Snyman, Lourens and old Sol started. The trauma and anxiety that was endured when the police investigated.

Then there was the fire of Sakkie Louw. The accusations, which were thrown around and followed by all the court cases.

We burn to survive, not to inflict damage on the land or the people. Who was here first our forefathers or Bosbou?

61. Heavens – Thank you- We've come a Long Way.

A Danie Ferreira story translated and retold by Cindy Oberholzer

Rose Cottage served as a school and a church.

Church services were held in the morning and then again in the evening, once a month. After the morning service we had a picnic under the Coral Trees. It was a lovely social family event. The black people also attended the same church, however they had to sit on the floor!

62. An Eccentric Person.

A Danie Ferreira story translated and retold by Cindy Oberholzer

Malan Dorfling, was an eccentric man. His name and phone number didn't appear in the telephone directory. He disliked visitors implicitly and didn't speak like a normal person. He had signs everywhere in his house saying: "Not so Loud" and "No loud speaking." His farms name was "Ry Verby" (Ride on Past).

He was the first person in the Valley to farm with Angora goats. My interest in Angora goats was great and I heard that he had a ewe to sell. His farm was in the mountains of the Grootrivierspoort. So I paid him a visit. The price was R50 per ewe, lambs were thrown in for free. I was thrilled. I took out my cheque book to pay.

"Would you like to post-date the cheque." He asked. I took up his offer and made the cheque payable in six months time.

Nine months passed and I noticed the cheque had not been honoured yet. He said: "I forgot."

He came to visit me on the farm. I asked him: "Would you like a stiff drink?"
His answer: "Yes beer, Castle". I had 24 bottles of beer a few in the fridge and a few on the shelf. I had one and he the other 23. Two at a time. One from the fridge and one from the shelf, in a long tall glass.

63. Did you Know?

A Danie Ferreira story translated and retold by Cindy Oberholzer

Rose Cottage, one of the oldest houses in the district, on the wall was the name SNYMAN in raised concrete, with the date underneath. This was later scraped off. I assume by the one and only Jannie Snyman when his tractor and the wall met by accident.

64. Making Fires is Not for "Sissies".

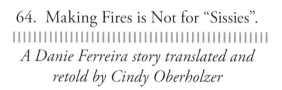

A Danie Ferreira story translated and retold by Cindy Oberholzer

Witberg, the modern farm of Sakkie Louw, at a stage was owned by Victor Brundston. He successfully grew wheat, however he loved to burn. With the wheat harvested and packed into stacks it was time to burn. Victor started the fire. Within seconds the fire spread to the neighbouring farms and into their mealie fields, which were days away from harvest. All went up in flames along with sheds, animals and a mill.

65. Wheat, Modernisation and Danger.

Danie Ferreira

From the earliest history grain and wheat were farmed here, with great success. The ground was fertile. The ripe wheat was harvested with sickles, dried, fastened with twine and piled into stacks. Then ridden to the thrashing floor, where it was trampled by horses, who went round and round.

Then along came the wood-thirsty steam engine. As children we loved it, as it was our job to pull straw bits out and scatter them. The engine was attached too and pulled by two oxen. Palmer sat behind the steam engine and smiled widely as it ran all day, like clockwork.
I asked him: "Oom. Why do you laugh all the time?"
His reply: "No. I am not laughing. I am just grinning."

Then along came a more modern 'thirsty' machine, it blew the straw out itself. No, no longer a steam engine, but a four cylinder petrol engine. The engine would hit a beat and miss a beat. Hit and miss, hit and miss as if to antagonise Oom Potgieter, who brought it from Alexander.

The engine ran and coughed, he tuned it here and tuned it there, but nothing helped. He removed the plugs and put the old ones back, with no luck. In the end he took a ten pound hammer and hit the machine that the sparks flew. This helped sometimes.

The Beautiful sight of Wheat, Wheat and more Wheat

And all the while the wheat was still being cut with a sickel.

Then along came a lucerne mower, on wheels. The damn thing made a huge noise. These mowers were called Tarka's. Two horses or two oxen were used to pull this mower.
My father decided to pull the Tarka with four mules instead. The mules were led by Natie, our worker. When the Tarka was attached and ready to go, as it moved forward it started to make a huge noise. The mules got such a fright from the noise they took off. Natie tried to calm the mules and hung on for dear life, with no luck. Natie was thrown under the mules and came to land in front of the cutter. The mules did not stop and the blade caught Natie under his chin and sliced his head off.

Occasionally, I still think of old Natie.

Some of the hard, enduring staff.

66. A Career in Jackal Hunting.

A Danie Ferreira story translated and retold by Cindy Oberholzer

The vermin and wiping them out.

The first jackal hunter employed here was William S, he did not receive a salary, however he could keep and sell the pelts. The Divisional Council paid £ 1 for a rooikat pelt. I once went with him to Lorrie to sell his wares, seven jackal pelts and one rooikat.

He was proud of what he brought home, he could pay for everything with enough left over for a small present for each of his children. For his son a pair of shoes. Gert was so proud of his shoes. However not long after they began to pinch his feet.

"Are your shoes pinching you?" asked Oom William.

"No Father, they fit perfectly."

Oom William pulled the sole of the shoe back and with his fingers felt inside and there we go, in the front of the shoe was a two inch nail, which was the culprit for the discomfort.

After William we established a Jackal club. The hunter was Piet van Rooyen. Thereafter was the irreplaceable Piet van Rooyen.
The premium which every farmer had to contribute was £ 3 per year. Piet van Rooyen made it possible for farmers to start farming with sheep. His salary was covered by the pelts and the £ 60 which the 20 members contributed. On occasions there would be a lot of moaning about the membership fees as some farmers had over 2000 morgan while others had only 500.

After Piet came a coloured guy by the name of Roelf. He was also extremely successful.

67. A Slip of the Tongue!

A Danie Ferreira story translated and retold by Cindy Oberholzer

Piet was fast asleep, when his cell phone woke him with a start. On the other end was Petrus from the farm.

Petrus said: "Boss, Boss, you must come to the farm immediately, here's now big trouble."

Piet says: "Petrus. What's the matter?"

Petrus: "Boss, Boss I know you are not going to believe me, but the ewe he had seven babies."

They realised that all the lambs will need to be hand reared with bottles. So Piet ends up at the chemist and asks: "Excuse me Mrs. But do you have "Lam Tiete?"

Without missing a beat she replied: "No, Sir, this is just a k@k bra !"

68. The Great Flood.

A Danie Ferreira story translated and retold by Cindy Oberholzer

24 March 1981 it started to rain, by the end of the 25 March, 17½ inches of rain had fallen (437.5ml). The Sand River and Bulk River's new bridges washed away.

The rain did not let up, every day, during April, May and June, finally in July it stopped. The flood was bigger than the floods of 1931 and 1932.

As fate would have it. Thereafter not a drop of rain for two years and in July 1983, yet again another flood!

Elands River –Flood of June 2011 - At the crossing to Mountain View (The Whiteheads)

69. Aunt Bettie.

A Danie Ferreira story translated and retold by Cindy Oberholzer

At Rose Cottage there was no organ to assist with the singing of the psalms. But we did have Aunt Bettie. She was the second wife of Oom Natie Ferreira, from The Fonteine.

She was a legend. She would sing from the front of the church. She would give the note and then begin to sing with us following after.

She was everything in one, an adviser, sick companion, midwife and doctor. People came from far and wide, in the middle of the night with their deadly sick children. She did everything, because she could do everything and was ready for any event. She never said no, with no payment or reward.

She became renowned for her unique handling of cancer, with great success she developed a plaster, which could draw the cancer out of the body. On occasions this would heal them or at least relieve the painful suffering.

Aunt Bettie died at The Fonteine. She died before her time, from a mastoid, which was an epidemic at that time. (I, myself suffered from a mastoid and if it wasn't for a successful operation, you would not be reading this).

After the death of Aunt Bettie it went sukkel – sukkel with the singing in the little church.

Around this time we got a new teacher, a Mrs. Lena Richbiter, she became known as the one who could 'throw a note'. Out of necessity the church bought an organ, with the first organist being Rinda Snyman and later Ada Scheepers.

70. The Ferreira's.

A Danie Ferreira story translated and retold by Cindy Oberholzer

Ignacio Ferreira was the original 'father' of the Ferreira's. He was born in 1696 and buried east of the Gouritz River in 1772, at 76yrs old.

71. A Little History.

A Danie Ferreira story translated and retold by Cindy Oberholzer

For many years the most well-known families of the Elands River were the Ferreiras, Wehmeyers, Snymans, Whiteheads, Scheepers and the Marais. During the early 1950's the Elands River was known as the 'Glory Years', as the production of wheat flourished. Money flowed into the valley. The Elands River was unique. Wheat was harvested year after year from the same lands. The rotation of crops were never considered and with this over cropping became the norm. The result was devastating.

By the time 2002 rolled in the well-known families were old or had completely 'disappeared'. Of the Ferreira family not one remained. Of the Snyman family no one and of the Wehmeyer two families remained and of the Scheepers just one.

72. The Establishment of Uitenhage and Surrounds.

A Danie Ferreira story translated and retold by Cindy Oberholzer

Before Uitenhage was established in 1799, the London Missionary Society was already doing missionary work along the Swartkops and Elands River. This was the start of the Rose Lane Church.

Kuils River Bridge – looking towards the (now) industrial area.

Rose Lane was first originally called The Union Chapel and was known as the mother of the Protestant Church, at the time. Besides the N.G. Kerk, which already existed for many years. These two churches were the only churches in Uitenhage and the surrounding areas.

In 1802 Commissioner General J.A Uitenhage De Mist proposed to the Cape Colony that they should take ownership of the area from the English.

In 1804, De Mist's daughter, son and himself took a tour through the Colony. He was so impressed by the choice of first pioneers whom had undertaken the task to farm the areas of Governor Van Der Graaff. That De Mist decided to form a town instead.

Uitenhage and its surrounds were then declared a town on the 25 April 1804 by Governor J.W. Jansens.

73. The Prices.

A Danie Ferreira story translated and retold by Cindy Oberholzer

Around 1830 everything was cheap, however although everything was cheap, money was scarce. The average price of a dairy cow was £2.00 (R4). The Doctor's fee, in town was 1/6d (15c) and in the area 3/- (30c) and a night call was 9/- (90c).

On the 3 July 1829 regulations were enforced with regards to the time the market could operate. Market hours 8.00 am to 10.00 am.

Around 1844 circumstances improved and things started looking up: Wheat price was 5/- per bushel (50c), barley and oats 2/- (20c), maize 3/- (30c), pea and beans 7/6, and potatoes 3/- (30c). Horses were £6 each, sheep 9/- (90c), goats 4/6, pigs £1 5s 0d each. Butter 4 pennies per lbs and 2d for a loaf of bread. Beef meat 1 1/2d per lbs and sheep meat 2d per lbs. Pork was expensive at – 7d per lbs.

74. The Names of Places.

A Danie Ferreira story translated and retold by Cindy Oberholzer

Back in the day the roads were difficult to navigate and the kloofs were exceptionally tricky, especially the Bulk and Sand Rivers as they were just mud holes. This is how the Bulk River got its name. From the 'Bulk" sound the oxen cried out, as they were under great strain, pulling the load up the steep kloof.

Other places names are: Verkeerdedrif (Wrong Drift), Rokoptel (Picking up Dress) Melkhoutboom (Milkwood Tree), Slangenhoekfontein (Snake Corner Fountain) (now known as Tip Tree), Kammievlei, Jobsekraal, Deyselskraal, De Fonteine (The Fountains), Cotswold, Doornhoek (Thorn Corner), Middelwater, Pereboom and Stilgenoeg (Quiet Enough).

75. The Natives.

A Danie Ferreira story translated and retold by Cindy Oberholzer

In 1856 the Natives became rebellious, again, and the Divisional Council had to see to it that the law was enforced. The Council had to notify all the locals of the situation and had to instruct the people of their duty as well as make sure they were ready for any situation that may arise.

In November 1856 an officer was appointed to every area. The Elands River was appointed with Captain A.A. Lange. He was later replaced by Mnr. J.L. Rautebach. On the 2 December 1856 a Mr. Michael A. Muller was elected as commander of all the burgers.

76. The Value of Homesteads.

A Danie Ferreira story translated and retold by Cindy Oberholzer

The value of homesteads in the Elands River in 1844 was nil. In 1859 it was £1400.00 per homestead. Up to 1860 tax was charged for the use of the roads, but no repairs were ever done. A large portion of the money collected was sent to the Western Province, to fix their farms.

After much research I never did find out when the Elands River Road was actually made. However the earliest record was that in early 1861 a Mr. A. Lange and twelve workers were appointed to repair the Elands River Road. The cost was £173 for about 50 miles (80km).

In 1866 a low water bridge was built over the Swartkops River in Uitenhage. Mr. Niven tendered £35 for the building of the bridge, however the Uitenhage Municipality would only pay £17 10s 0d.

77. Relentless Disasters.

A Danie Ferreira story translated and retold by Cindy Oberholzer

On the 9th February **1869**. The thermometer reached 139 degrees Fahrenheit (59 degrees celsius). This was the day of the great fire, from Swellendam to Alexandria. How it began, no one knows, perhaps crystal stones or shards of a broken bottles reflection in the sun. The entire Southern Cape was in flames. Fires started in numerous places simultaneously.

The veld was bone dry and the farmers, farmworkers, kraals, sheds livestock and wild life all succumbed to the fire. Everything was destroyed. Many districts, Mosselbay, Knysna, Humansdorp, Elands River, Uitenhage, the outskirts of Port Elizabeth to Alexandria were burned to the ground.
Ox wagon and horse carts were all consumed. In the Uitenhage and Elands River districts people had to flee from the fire. Some folk from the Elands River told tales of having to stay submerged in water up to their necks, to stay alive.

In **1873** was the greatest drought ever. There was just no grazing at all. Livestock died by the thousands. This devastation was followed by an outbreak of horse sickness - where horses died in their stables. Thereafter horses and mules were scarce and expensive – the price shot up from £40 to £50 each.

In **1876** was the Great Flood, which washed the roads away. The then Council could not repair the roads. A certain Mr. Paterson was appointed to start the repairs and maintenance of the roads, mainly the roads on the outskirts. His budget was £ 2 250 per year.

In **1877** was another depression, this was one of the hardest years in history of Uitenhage drought times. The dams dried up, the veld was parched. Warm berg winds blew for months. Prayer hours were held but still the earth turned black from the fires. Cattle collapsed and died by the hundreds. As usual, due to the conditions, horse sickness ran amok. Some farmers lost everything.

In **1880** things started looking up after seven years of hardship, droughts and depression. Rains fell shortly after each other and with this the harvests were successful and bountiful. The livestock were in excellent condition and the prices were high. Crop prices also improved. Oxen instead of horses or mules were used for ploughing work, with the result beef prices became scarce and meat prices rose. Ostrich farming was profitable. Marino sheep and Angora Goats were imported from Asia Minor and farmed here. The working population increased and so did the worker's wages. However poverty amongst the labourers still loomed large in the Uitenhage and surrounding districts.

From **1895** to **1898** the Rinderpest broke out amongst the cattle and almost killed them all.

From **1899** to **1902**. Martial Law. A ban on the movement of people was instituted. Church services and bazaars in the outlying areas came to a standstill. Then in 1900 the Anglo-Boere-War broke out. Only the two Republics – The Transvaal and the Orange Free State were involved with the fight against England, but here in the Elands River the divide was felt. Nobody trusted anybody. National Scouts, Joiners, were the order of the day. Farmer against Farmer. During General Smuts's invitation of the 'Colonies' the Elands River was believed to have provided horses to the Smuts commando.

From **1914** to **1918** was the First World War. The heart sore, which is still raw, from the war, lays in a shallow memory of what happened to the loved ones, 'the brothers', who had fallen and families still suffering as they were used as fodder.

In **1918** the Spanish Flu hit the Elands River, which did not spare anyone. Many, from all races, died here.

1929 was the start of the depression years. To make matters worse the Eastern Cape fell into a serious drought – money became non-existent. There were farms and neighbouring districts, who had no grazing or water. The Elands River managed to survive through this period, as the area had odd bits of rains fell.

From all over, farmers who had lost their farms, came to the Elands River Valley in search of farms or little pieces of land in the hopes of striking a deal, to find a place to stay or a piece of land to graze their starving cattle.

The results were not good for the local community. Animal sicknesses and parasites, which were unknown in the area, were assumed to have been brought in from Murraysburg.

From **1941** to **1942** was a time for horse sickness. I was farming at that time at High Water. Our entire team of mules and horses died. My nephew C.D. Ferreira had to drag our last horse "Tommie", away with his car and bury him.

78. "You only come across Men and Women like the Voortrekkers once in a Lifetime"

A Danie Ferreira story translated and retold by Cindy Oberholzer

1938: The Great Trek, 100 year remembrance day, took place in Uitenhage. Five jaw boned wagons, from various districts, trekked from Uitenhage to Pretoria Voortrekker Monument, as it did many years before. On the 10th September 1938, the Voortrekker wagons arrived at Andries Pretorius in Uitenhage. This was an extraordinary event. The mayor, Mr. M C Curry, addressed the crowd, and welcomed everyone. His message in English was memorable and touching.

The mode of transport – ox wagons.

The driver of the Red Afrikaner team of oxen was Hekkie Ferreira. The 'family' on the wagon were: HS Smit (Father), Mrs. W Palen (Mother), Old father Lemmer (Grandfather) and the children, Maryna Oosthuisen, Muraal Terblanche, Gustave Smit and last but not least the youngster on the wagon, in a pair of flap trousers and all, was me, Danie Ferreira, from the Elands River.

The terrain that was crossed, with the ox wagons.

79. The "Modern" Postal Service.

A Danie Ferreira story translated and retold by Cindy Oberholzer

After Captain, the postman, the post was delivered with a regular postal service, once a week. This was the start of the Posting bags (a canvas bag with one's name embossed on a metal tag), which were dropped off at your gate, by horse cart and later a motor car.

The first motor car, which rode the post in, was owned by Uncle Fanie Heyns of the Elands River. Later a truck was set into service. This was a great help as the truck could collect and take egg crates, butter crates, mealies and potatoes back to the market.

The first regular truck service was owned by Hadly Hawkins (alias Zip Snyman).

80. Money System.

A Danie Ferreira story translated and retold by Cindy Oberholzer

1814 – 1826 : Money was scarce, under the management of Lord Charles Somerset. More and more paper money was in the system, which had very little value. The pennie was the common money at the time. Its value in 1806 - 4/2 shillings and lost its value till it finally settled at 1/6. In 1825 the British stepped in and decided that the British monetary system would be used. This was an excellent decision. However the money lenders and property owners were hit hard as the value of money and property plummeted.

81. The Market.

A Danie Ferreira story translated and retold by Cindy Oberholzer

The market was the meeting place for all, at the time. The lekker coffee at sunrise in the early morning, the conversation, the echoing of the auctioneer: "…por, por, tjieling…..por, por…..tjieling…". Everyone understood.

82. Piet – The Hunter.

A Danie Ferreira story translated and retold by Cindy Oberholzer

James Bennington farmed at Tip Tree. One day we heard the jackal calling. My wife skin crawled with goose bumps. Piet, James and myself took our dogs and picked up the trail at Tafelberg. For miles we followed the dogs and jackals till behind the Shonga mountains. The dogs lost the scent and we had to turn back. Somehow, under our noses, the jackal had turned back. Piet picked up the trail again and the dogs lead us all the way back to the Tafelberg where we started our journey.

We heard the dog's 'tjaf' at a certain point and then as we walked on – nothing, when we came back over that spot, then they began to 'tjaf' again. The jackal was underground.

Piet took off his jacket and dropped himself into the hole. Minutes later, the dogs and a bushpig came piling out the hole. The barking and crying of the dogs became still. Piet had vanished for what felt like an eternity, to later appear from the hole, feet first dragging a dead jackal. Piet did not have an ounce of fear.

On another occasion, somewhere near Doringkraal, Piet and his dogs picked up a scent of a leopard and after an intense chase, they chased the leopard up a tree. Piet and his shepherd, were both unarmed. The leopard was cornered and aggressive as it prepared to pounce. Piet grabbed the shepherd's staff and pinned the leopard in the v of the tree, and asked the shepherd to run back and get his gun.

I repeat ... not an ounce of fear!

Some of the old hunters.

George Whitehead Senior and friends with a Leopard.
Hunting in the valley. The bugger wasbringing back what you shot.

83. The Brothers Who Married the Sisters.

A Danie Ferreira story translated and retold by Cindy Oberholzer

Grandpa Tossie's two brothers, Cornelius and Hansie, married the two Lubbe sisters, Hester and Anna, from the concentration camp in Uitenhage. Thereafter they all moved and farmed in Philipalos.

84. The Jackal Club.

A Danie Ferreira story translated and retold by Cindy Oberholzer

After Piet, the next jackal hunter was Roelf and after Roelf, Lourens.

And all of a sudden there were no more vermin. The Council, with the spokesperson being Mr. Crause, held a meeting at Verkeerdedrif, to discuss the fact that no pelts where being brought in. Therefore there was no longer a need for the Jackal Club. A vote was taken with only two votes against closing the club. The club was officially disbanded.

There was no need for the farmers to worry about the Jackals any longer as small livestock farming was no longer popular at the time, instead wheat was the future.

85. My First Day at Brandwag High School.

A Danie Ferreira story translated and retold by Cindy Oberholzer

1937: For me it was farewell to my little farm school, with its handful of children. So with great excitement and trepidation we arrived at Brandwag High School for the first day of school. "Chaos". The first few days we sat in front of the school and even spilled into the street, there were so many children. The standard six's, seven's and eight's were sorted and divided into classes.

86. Wheat.

A Danie Ferreira story translated and retold by Cindy Oberholzer

"It was the best of times, it was the worst of times." Even though it was said by Charles Dickens in 1850, 100 years later in 1950 was it relevant to the Elands River Valley.

This was the time of building the wheat industry. Our lands, which for decades were not productive, were ploughed over. It was a sight for sore eyes to see field of lands planted with wheat. The yield was astounding.

Forty harvested bags per one seed bag was a failure, however the yield shot up to one hundred bags per one seed bag.

The time of the sickle, the self-binding and the threshing-machine were gone forever. Now it was the time of the poachers, drifters and the tractors that droned day in and day out.

Grazing lands were rooigras, which used to grow safely on the edges. Small livestock grazed at leisure. Now all ploughed over and almost overnight wheat lands stood in its place.

This was a magnificent sight and something to see first-hand. First the ploughed lands and then a green carpet.

We established a wheat Co-Op in Uitenhage and a branch in Humansdrop. Wilhelm Snyman was unanimously chosen as Director of the Elands River District.

Railway busses transported the wheat to the Co-Op. The Co-op could not keep up with the supply, as it didn't have enough storage facilities for the wheat. Tension ran between friends. One would book a bus from the Co-op. Then wait for hours only to hear that your neighbour intercepted the transport and had already done two loads. The lesson was you did not book a load with the Co-op but instead with the driver!

The next day my bus arrived. The driver's name was Blompot (Flowerpot). I sent my workers for breakfast.

"No we must first load" said Blompot.

"We have plenty of time, we have been waiting for three days now, why the hurry." I said.

We loaded the bus.

"Tomorrow I will come again to load another load." said Blompot.

"I do not believe you." I said.

"Man I am so scared of cancer, if I don't come tomorrow then God must give me cancer." said Blompot.

Blompot did not come.

Fields of wheat upon fields of wheat were magnificently harvested. But then, small ant hills began to break out in the fields, especially in the new fields. "Not to worry." Said the men in the know. They are just ant hills. Well they turned out not to be ant hills but vrot pootjie, in English "take all disease".

The writing was on the wall. It was the start of the end.

Then we planted barley. Beer barley didn't get "take all disease" or didn't get infected with rust. The grade was good and the colour was great. The yield per hectare was greater than that of wheat. The prices were also right. The glory days continued.

Greater combiners, modern tractors, new cars, new bakkies streamed into the valley. Salesmen from all over came a-calling, fertilizer representatives, assurance salesmen, insurance salesmen and many more.

Landbou technical services descended on us. They knew better. We had to open offices, use a variety of equipment, use more pesticides and so on and so on.

After all the years of hardship is was great to be able to breathe a little, in the time of plentiful.

87. The Ferreira's.

A Danie Ferreira story translated and retold by Cindy Oberholzer

17 May **1722**. The ship, The Chantes, was ship wrecked on a beach, near the Castle, in Cape Town. This ship and many others, which belonged to the Dutch East Indian Company suffered the same fate that night in a huge storm. The loss of lives totalled 660.

Only two of the 70 people on The Chantes drowned. Of the remaining 70 one was Ignacio Ferreira. Forefather of every Ferreira in South Africa (born 1695).

Ignacio decided to remain in the Cape in the service of the Duch East Indian Company as a soldier.

In **1725** Ignacio hired himself out as a 'slave' to resident Goetehuis. In the contract between Goetehuis and Ignacio, Ignacio promised to be loyal in his service as 'slave'. For the sum of 12 Cape Dutch florin, 1 pound of tobacco, alcohol and accommodation.

On the 6th November **1735**, after being a bachelor till he was 40 years old, Ignacio got married to an 18 year old young lady, Martha Terblanche.

From around **1748**, at 53 years old, Ignacio started his farming and on the 28 March 1748 he bought his first sheep farm "Hartebees". It was 60 morgen – his first piece of land.

Around **1762** Ignacio was a proud owner of 6 horses, 80 cattle, 600 sheep, a fancy cock, a bible and a pistol.

Ignacio had ten children, but we will only concentrate on the sixth child.
Thomas Ignacio Ferreira:

Thomas Ignacio Ferreira, born **1743** and died in **1814** (71 years old). In **1776**, at 33 years old, Thomas moved close to Papenkuilsfontein in Algoa Bay, where he became one of the first white pioneers of that time. He was a member of the expedition which in **1782** searched for the survivor of the shipwrecked ship, the Governor. On his farm was the first defence structure established for the security of the Eastern Border and for a time he was in charge of Fort Frederick in Algoa Bay.

The Ferreira's are of strong origin, made from tough genes and the proof is if you look under any rock in the Elands River and Patense areas you will find a Ferreira.

88. The Murder.

A Danie Ferreira story translated and retold by Cindy Oberholzer

Martha Ferreira was the daughter of Thomas Ferreira, she was known as 'angry' Martha. Martha was charged with the murder of her slave, Marissa. She apparently used to beat her with a sjambok daily, to the point that one day she beat her so that Marissa lost an eye. Not long after this Marissa died.

From the transcript of the court case, which was held in George, 'angry' Martha was described as: "A woman bearing all the appearance of a better than ordinary farmer's education." During the trial the infamous Coenraad de Buys testified against her. He was a white outlaw who lived in Gaika's kraal as a native.

She was found not guilty on all charges against her.

In 1811 Van der Kemp and Reid, from the London Mission Station, made a list and sent it to the Church in London. The list was a list of accusations of over 100 murders of white people committed by Hottentot, in the Uitenhage district, and that the governor and magistrate would not investigate. (In 1803, Bethalsdorp had already made a list of charges against the Hottentot for murders committed and not investigated in that area).

Sir John Cradock was then instructed to investigate the murder charges. Judge's Cloete and Struberg, from the renegade court, was ordered to hear all the cases in 1812.

No charges of murder were proved and in fact the investigation ultimately discovered that the farmers, on the whole, treated their workers fairly and with respect.

89. Cradock and Graham.

A Danie Ferreira story translated and retold by Cindy Oberholzer

1811 to 1814. Sir John Cradock replaced Graaff van Caledon as Governor of the Cape. Graham was appointed as Cradock's representative in the Eastern Region, to safeguard the residents against the robberies and murders by the natives.

These were not good times. Graham set up armed border posts and guards had to track and retrieve stolen livestock. If they could not they had to shoot the native's cattle and destroy their vegetable gardens.

This is how Graham cleaned up the the area.

90. The Land System.

A Danie Ferreira story translated and retold by Cindy Oberholzer

In **1813**, Cradock changed the Land Laws. The farmers in the Elands River could get permits to lend money, in order to own their own farms. Cradock gave the farmers the permission to put the farms in their own names, as long as they went through the registered process and paid for all the fees which were incurred. They could then get maps and the title deeds. One of the consequences of the Great Trek was that the farmers did not receive their title deeds or maps even after they were allocated and the land measured up.

In other words there were no owners of the land before 1813 in the Elands River.

91. The Slave Proclamation.

A Danie Ferreira story translated and retold by Cindy Oberholzer

In 1823 Somerset set in motion the slave proclamation:

1. Slaves had to be registered.
2. All slave children had to go to school.
3. Slaves could marry.
4. Slave families had to be sold together.
5. Work hours were established at 10 hours in the winter and 12 hours per day in the summer.
6. Working days – seven per week.

92. Somerset!

A Danie Ferreira story translated and retold by Cindy Oberholzer

While Donkin was out from India on holiday, he assisted Somerset in 1820 with government matters. Somerset was meant to pay Donkin a salary of £ 5 000, however he only received £ 3 000. The other £ 2 000 - gone!

In 1826, Somerset was dismissed from his post, due to 'absurd' accusations which surfaced.

93. Pay your Debt!

A Danie Ferreira story translated and retold by Cindy Oberholzer

Adriaan van Jaarsveld borrowed a sum of money from the bank. He got behind with his payments. He paid timeously up to 1791, however by 1798 he started to complain that his payments were not coming off. He produced a receipt, which stated he had paid up to December 1794. He had changed the 1 to a 4. His fraud had been discovered. He was charged and had to appeared in court, he did not pitch. He was rearrested and was escorted under police guard to Cape Town.

When Willem Prinsloo got wind of this. He rallied about 40 burgers together, formed a posse and sprung van Jaarsveld free.

General Dandag sent a troop of English soldiers to Graaff Reinett to capture the, now bandits. Van Jaarveld, Prinsloo and the burgers could not withstand the onslaught and the soldiers captured Van Jaarsveld and Prinsloo. They were sentenced to death, however the judgement was not carried out.

Van Jaarsveld was instead taken prisoner and was kept at the Castle jailhouse in Cape Town were he ultimately died.

94. Mrs. Uys.

A Danie Ferreira story translated and retold by Cindy Oberholzer

1837: A Farmer, Piet Uys, (leader of the Uys Trek) travelled from the Uitenhage District to Cape Town for business.

While he was away his wife, Mrs. Uys, reprimanded her maid. The maid, Miss. Villiers, proceeded to lay a charge at the Uitenhage Magistrates court against her, for hitting her.

Mrs. Uys was summoned to appear in court. She asked her father-in-law for help by accompanying her to court, which he immediately agreed to.

Mrs. Uys asked the magistrate: "Why are you treating me like a criminal. I did not commit any crime?"

The magistrate answered with a question: "Do you know with whom you are speaking? Do you know that I sit on the seat of Moses?"

With this the father-in-law asked if he could say a few words: "Your Honour my daughter has no knowledge of the seat of Moses. But I know very well that the seat is honourable, righteous and impartial. Yet how you still sitting on the seat, I don't know."

When Piet Uys returned and heard of his wife's ordeal, he decided to pack his family and bags and move to a 'new land'.

95. The Church.

A Danie Ferreira story translated and retold by Cindy Oberholzer

We built a beautiful little church in 1950, in the Elands Valley. At the very first service my daughter was christened, Petra Aneen Ferreira. Ds. Fullard was the preacher that day.

Rose Cottage Church – 1950

25 years later, at the same church with the same preacher, Ds. Fullard, who came out specially for the occasion as it was to commemorate the church turning 25 and also to christening of my daughter, Petra's, daughter Leandra.

Petra was also married in the very same church.

96. Thinking Back.

A Marie Heyns story retold by Cindy Oberholzer

The people in the Valley have always had concern for each other. In 1970 the Women's Action group was established. The idea was to meet once a month to arrange demonstrations, walks, bible studies and to serve sweet treats at functions and funerals. Once a year the Women's Group also arranged the church bazaar. All new comers were welcomed by the ladies and the ladies were invited to become a member of the Women's Action and become part of the community.

The people cared and when someone needed a tractor fixed or if someone was sick, there was always someone to help.

On voting day all the different party's representatives met in the morning to make sure that all was in order and that the day would go smoothly, by that afternoon everyone would get together to have snacks and share a few jokes.

What a privilege it was to have a farm school, our children could attend school till standard 5, still living in their own homes. Aunty Fienie Snyman used her Kombi to transport the school children to and from school. They had excellent teachers who taught the children and prepared them for high school. The school was at "Cotswold" the name of the school was "Balemre" – the name of the huge tree, which grew there.

The Elands River people were generous, if you ever popped in, you would be offered a plate of food. One day we were returning from a Boere Function held in Uitenhage. The council was busy repairing the road at the Bulk River, it had been raining continuously and when we tried to climb the steep hill with the Isuzu, we stood dead still in the mud, not moving an inch. We knocked at the Van Rensburg's door. It was 1.00am and in true Elands style we were invited to stay the night.

97. Van Stadens Bridge Jumpers.

A Marie Heyns story retold by Cindy Oberholzer

One day someone jumped off the Van Stadens Bridge. It was tragic, shocking news. Then I heard Koekoe (Danie Ferreira) over the farm radio: "It is so high I will stand on my hands to jump back up!"

Marie Heyns

98. Three-Feet (Jakob) with his Lots to Say.

A Marie Heyns story retold by Cindy Oberholzer

I said to Three-Feet one day: "Time is running past so fast. It was just Christmas and now it is Christmas again! I don't know if I will see next Christmas, maybe I will not be alive."

Three - Feet replied: "Are you at least ready to go? I am ready to go, my 'good points' are more than my 'bad points'!"

99. The Commando's.

A Marie Heyns story retold by Cindy Oberholzer

When the army came to explain the rules of the Commandos, in the beginning the ladies were a little afraid, however we quickly became interested. We learned how to shoot an "R1" rifle, read a compass and how to communicate. It was good to learn how to react in an emergency situation.

100. The Whiteheads of Elands River.

Jenny Eldridge

Frederick Whitehead (Senior):

Afdak, the original Whitehead farm, was granted to General Cuyler in 1818, thereafter it was owned by Mr Lange in 1835 and then hired to Mr. Muller, who is buried on the present Gumdale. It then passed on to Mr. Johnson and Mr. Snyman.

Frederick Whitehead (Senior)

Afdak is bordered on the South by the Elandsberg, to the North by the Shonga Mountains (Groendal), to the East by the Bulk River and to the West, by Keurkloof.

Frederick Whitehead (Senior) came to the valley in the late 1800's and went to work for Mr. Palmer at Rose Cottage (Wheatlands). He married Cornelia Ferreira (born 1866) from Tip Tree in 1889. They bought Afdak, but Cornelia didn't want to live on the homestead as it was too close to the road, so they built their home on the present Forest Glade.

Cornelia Ferreira.

They had five children: George Ferreira Whitehead (Senior) was born at Rose Cottage in 1890 and four more children were born at Forest Glade, Noel Rupert (1891), Stephanie (1893), Alfred (who died of heart problems), Frederick and Charles Ellis (1903).

Cornelia only lived till she was 45 and died around 1916. Nellie Tauber was then employed to teach the children. An inspector would come to the farm to test the children, to see if they had passed or not.

Nellie and Frederick (Senior) where later married. She was a very stern lady and also very house proud, to the extent that the walls around the house had to be whitewashed weekly. The bedrooms all had "Hemelbedde" (four poster beds) much to the delight of the grandchildren. I remember her from when I was a child and found her very intimidating.

The Whiteheads – George, Noel, Stephanie, Frederick and Ellis.

George Whitehead (Senior):

My grandfather, George Whitehead (Senior), was at Muir College and when it was school holidays his father would send horses to fetch them from school. They would ride back over the mountains (a road connected Kruis River to Mountain View). The boys were issued with live carbines and ammunition, as they were in the "cadets" at Muir. On the way home from Uitenhage, they used to do a bit of hunting and only got home late in the evenings.

Some of the Karoo boys would go home on horseback.

My grandfather, George (Senior), could not get on with his strict step-mother, Nellie, and so went to farm at Mountain View, in about 1906.

The Whiteheads – Frederick, Nellie, Ellis, Amelia and Unknown

The farm Afdak was divided into: Forest Glade, Mountain View, Gumdale, Afdak Outspan and Keurkloof. The official demarcation was made in 1936. The Meadows (near Sand River Dam) was purchased later.

101. Keurkloof.

Jenny Eldridge

After the death of Frederick Whitehead, Stephanie, his only daughter, inherited the farm. Stephanie was born in 1893 and married Sidney Ferreira, from Gamtoos, they were living in Pietermaritzburg at the time. Their two children were born in Pietermaritzburg, Monica in 1919 and Freddy in 1930. Monica was 14 when they returned to Keurkloof. The children attended Peerboom although later Monica returned to Pietermaritzburg where she matriculated and Freddy went to Doringhoek on horseback and later to Brandwag.

The, out of commission, original water pipeline, from the Sand River Dam to Port Elizabeth, running through Keurkloof and Mountain View.

Monica married Gerhardus Coenrad Wehmeyer in 1942 and they farmed at Verkeerdedrift, where their two children were born Arista in 1944 and Ewald a few years later. Arista now lives in Somerset West and Ewald farms at Tip Tree. Ewald married Cecile Lottering in 1979 and they have two children Coenraad and Liezel.

The, out of commission, original water pipeline, from the Sand River Dam to Port Elizabeth, running through Keurkloof and Mountain View.

After school, Freddy joined his father to farm, at Keurkloof. In 1944 he married Stella Cowie and they had two children Madelein and Maynard. The family then moved to Zambia, where they farmed for 5 years, returning to Keurkloof to farm until the 1970's. Thereafter he sold the farm and lived in Uitenhage.

The farm has changed hands many times and is now owned by Carston Clotz.

102. Mountain View.

Jenny Eldridge

George Whitehead (Senior)

George Whitehead (Senior), my grandfather, was still fairly young when he came to Mountain View. He built himself a wattle and daub house on the South side of the Elands River where the present citrus orchard is. Here he farmed and started building the homestead, which was completed in 1912. The homestead still stands today, although it has been altered over the years.

In 1914, George married Catherine Elizabeth Maria (Katie as she was known, she was born in 1893), from Bergplaas, which is at the very top of the valley. After their marriage they came to live at Mountain View.

Four days after being married and living at Mountain View a remarkable event took place, as Katie helped save a man's life. The Port Elizabeth Municipality was building a bridge across the Elands River, to take the pipe line from the Sand River Dam. The foreman in charge was involved in a terrible accident and lost three fingers on his one hand. He was bleeding profusely and had lost an enormous amount of blood, he was in huge trouble. Katie knew, if the bleeding did not stop soon, he would die. She remembered her mother's old poultice remedy (grated potato and vinegar) to stop bleeding. She took a chance and applied this to the desperate foreman's hand. The bleeding stopped. She made arrangements with the neighbouring farmer to take him to the Port Elizabeth hospital. The journey took 6 hours, by horse and cart. He lived !

Mr. J. C. MacAdam, care taker at the Sand River Dam, told the Port Elizabeth City Engineer of the remarkable event and in recognition of her good deed, presented her with a telephone. The first in the valley. The telephone was invaluable as it became a life line on many occasions during floods and other emergencies. The telephone still hangs in the house today.

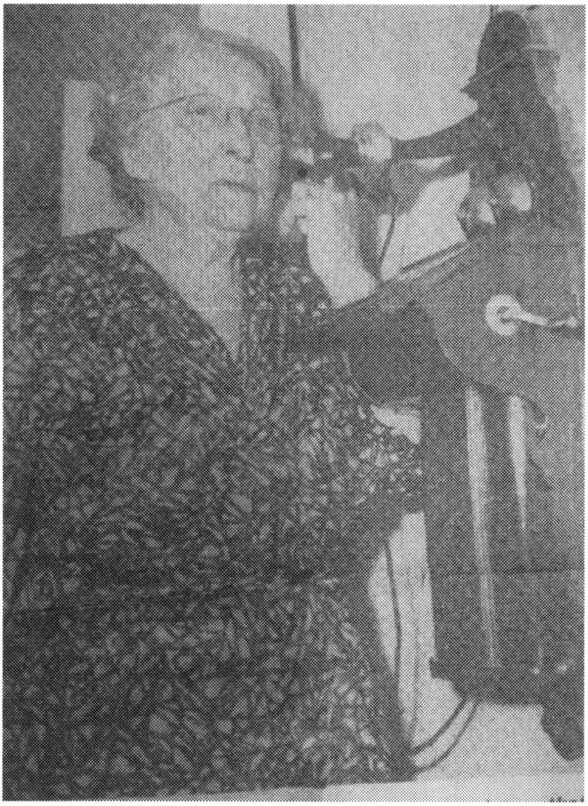

Katie Whitehead with the phone.

George Whitehead (Senior), farmed with fruit and vegetables and did very well in the war years supplying the ships and exporting oranges. The produce had to be taken to market in Uitenhage by ox wagon, this took two days. They would outspan the oxen and overnight in Uitenhage, before their return journey. He would also run cattle into the mountains, which he hired from the then Department of Forestry, he would then have to trek on horseback to check on the cattle, overnight in the mountains and return the next day.

The phone today – still hanging in the same spot.

George Whitehead (Senior) had three children: Frederick Stanley (Junior) (known as Stanley), my father, (1915), Shiela Hilda (1918) and George Solomon (Junior) (1924).

Katie was a very hard working lady. One of her many chores was to stoke the steam engine, which pumped water from the river to water the crops. She used to take baby Stanley in his basket and lay him under the pear tree, near the engine. He was very content and slept most of the time, no doubt because of the soothing sound of the steam engine.

On another occasion, it was extremely cold and wet. George (Senior), was in the mountains and Katie grew more and more concerned for the angora goats in the freezing weather. Unable to think of any other solution, she brought them into the house and kept them there until the weather improved. The goats all survived but it took many days of hard labour to get the house clean again.

When my Uncle George (Junior) was about 5 years old, George (Senior) before going away, gave instructions for the cattle to be dipped. Sadly the worker made the dip mixture too strong and the cattle were so severely burnt that they had to be shot. Needless to say George (Senior), was furious and the boy was severely punished, in turn the worker felt the punishment was too harsh and vowed to punish him in turn. One day when George (Senior) was away, he snuck up to the house and threw a stone through the window, which hit the maid on the head. She was okay, but when the worker saw Katie with a the shot gun, he fled. Katie covered the stone with a skottle, to protect the evidence and notified the Tip Tree police. They came the next day with police dogs and made all the workers lie on the grass. The dogs sniffed the stone and then the boys. The dogs picked out the guilty one.

George (Senior) was "Justice of the Peace" and so was responsible for registering births and deaths. He was once called upon to investigate a body that had been found in the mountains. He went up on horseback and on checking the body could not find any marks. They decided to bury the man on the spot and it was recorded that he died from a snake bite. No one ever enquired about him.

George (Senior) and Katie's Golden Wedding Anniversary.

George (Senior) and Katie were true settlers and much loved by the folks in the Valley and especially by his family. George (Senior) died in 1964 and Katie lived on her own on the homestead. The children kept Granny Katie company in the evenings, when they were home from school. She was very nervous being on her own at night. She died in 1973 at the age of 80.

Frederick Stanley Whitehead (Junior) – Stanley:

My father, Stanley, after completing school, went to Saarsveld in George to study forestry for a year or two. He than came home to Mountain View to farm with his father, George (Senior) on one half of the farm. He met and married my mother Rhona Mackay from Port Elizabeth (born 1921) who was nursing at the time. Stanley farmed with fruit, vegetables and bees. In those years he had abundant harvests. Stanley built the farm house in 1945, where I presently live. Stanley had two children: Me - Jennifer (born 1944) (known as Jenny) and Allan George (born 1947).

Stanley and Rhona Whitehead on their Wedding day.

Jenny and Allan Whitehead:

We attended boarding school from a very early age, I went to Riebeek College and Allan to Muir College in Uitenhage. After matriculating I studied and worked at the SAIMR, in Port Elizabeth and qualified as a Medical Technologist specialising in Haemotalogy. Allan went to the army for 9 months and then onto Rhodes University to study.

Jenny Eldridge (nee Whitehead)

I worked for another year after qualifying and then decided to spread my wings and see a bit of Europe. I left aboard the Windsor Castle sailing to South Hampton. On the first day out from Cape Town, I met Trevor Eldridge who was returning to London after spending four years in Zambia. We had a wonderful voyage and after arriving in London we kept up our friendship. I worked at the Middlesex Hospital and after touring Europe for three months I moved to South London where Trevor lived.

At that time he was working for Lloyds Bank. We got engaged and married in 1969. After spending another year in London we emigrated to Rhodesia where we spent fourteen wonderful years. We were in Salisbury when Nicola Kim (born 1974) and Jason Douglas (born 1975) were born. We later moved to Bulawayo. Life in Rhodesia even with war, sanctions and convoys, was wonderful. It is a beautiful country and let's hope it will one day return to its former glory.

My mother, Rhona, passed away in 1973 at the age of 52, a few months before Nicola was born. She was a wonderful person and had a very hard life with no electricity, an outside loo and a donkey to heat water. She never complained and still managed to have a lovely garden.

My father remarried an old friend Doreen Frost and they continued to farm on Mountain View. After the death of my Grandmother Katie, in 1973 (a few months before my mother), the farm was divided between my father, Stanley and his brother, George Soloman (Senior).

In 1984, because of the deteriorating education system, we moved to Johannesburg and settled in Brackenhurst/Alberton. We lived there for sixteen years, where the children finished their education. Trevor worked for Dions and Game as an internal auditor and later as Regional admin manager. Every year we returned to Zimbabwe for a holiday, Trevor and Jason to fish at Lake Kariba and myself to visit relatives. We also managed to get down to Mountain View once a year, it was always good to see the family and Trevor and the children loved the farm as much as I did.

In 2000, Trevor was offered a post at Game – Port Elizabeth. We were delighted as my father, Stanley, had left me the house after he died in 1999 (aged 84) and Allan the farm. We moved down in the June but sadly my step-mother, Doreen, had died a few days before. Jason followed a few months later and Nicole remained in Johannesburg. Unfortunately Trevor died in the November after a short struggle with cancer. I am still on the farm and hope I will never have to move.

Allan Whitehead:

Allan met his wife Brenda Sprenger (born 1949) while they were both studying for B.SC degrees at Rhodes. Brenda grew up in Queenstown and went to school at Girls High School, Queenstown.

Allen and Brenda on their Wedding day.

They both moved to Uitenhage were Allan taught Maths and Science at Muir and Brenda taught at Riebeek College. They married in Stutterheim in 1976. In 1974, Allan bought the mountain farm Vermont, where he farmed with cattle. Still teaching and farming he sold Vermont in 1984 and bought Orange Grove, which is adjacent to Mountain View. In 1996 he retired from teaching.

George Soloman Whitehead (Senior):

George (Senior) (born 1924), my uncle, married Merle Barnette and had one daughter, Rosemary. They divorced after a few years and he remarried Dulcie Heeger (nee Prinsloo), who had three children from her previous marriage: Sandra, Rodney and René. George (Senior) and Dulcie had one son of their own, George Neil Arther (Junior). They lived in Uitenhage and George (Senior) worked at Goodyear. Young George (Junior) went to Muir College and then to U.P.E. to study Geology. He pulled out after a few years and had many interesting jobs until he decided to become an insurance broker. George (Senior) inherited the other section of Mountain View when my Grandmother, Katie, died and it became a weekend retreat more than a farm. George (Senior) and Dulcie were ill for many years. Dulcie died in 1986 and George (Senior) in 1988. (aged 64)

George Neil Arthur Whitehead (Junior):

George (Junior) married Sharon Simms and they had two children: Shaniel (born 1986) and Daniel (born 1990). They were divorced in 1992 and in 2000 George (Junior) remarried Anneka Mattheus (nee van Vuuren), who had two children from her previous marriage: Janus and Anina. George (Junior) and Anneke had one son of their own, David George (born 2002). When George (Senior) died George (Junior) inherited the farm, where he farms with sheep and cattle. He has built onto the old house and it is much improved after standing empty for many years. George (Junior) had also built a few log cabins on the farm, which he hires out to hikers and 4 x 4 enthusiasts. He has also made numerous hiking trails for the visitors to enjoy the beautiful natural fauna and flora.

George (Junior) and Anneka Whitehead.

103. Forest Glade.

Jenny Eldridge

Charles Ellis (known as Ellis):

Forest Glade was the original farm and homestead where the Whiteheads grew up and when Frederick (Senior) died in 1935, it was farmed by his youngest son Ellis.
Ellis married Elsabie du Preez in 1940 and they lived in one of the out-buildings, which was then added on over the years and is still used today. They had six children: Elmarie (born 1941), Yvonne (born 1944), Marlene (born 1947), Stephanie (born 1948), Elvidge Ellis and Helene (born 1953).

Ellis suffered from a hereditary heart disease that was passed down from the Ferreira's, many of the children were affected. Helene had a hole in the heart, Yvonne and Marlene both had pacemakers, this disease has been passed on to the next generation.

They were an extremely happy family and as children we used to visit often, walking between Mountain View and Forest Glade. Elsabie was a wonderful lady, a good cook and always had a smile and a welcome, even with such a large family. Ellis was bedridden for many years and Elsabie ran the farm.

Once when the workers were irrigating the lands (ou lande), the Avance two-stroke engine was pumping the water. They noticed that the engine was running faster and faster. They tried switching it off and banging it – to no avail. The connecting pipe broke and it took off into the bushes where it finally came to rest. It was repaired by my father, Stanley, who used it for many years. The exhaust is still being used on Allan's (my brother) pump!

The girls all married and moved away, Elmarie to Postmansburg, Yvonne to Uitenhage and to the Western Cape, Marlene to Port Elizabeth and then to Johannesburg, Stephanie to Alexandria, Helene to Johannesburg and Elvidge to Uitenhage.

Elvidge Whitehead:

Elvidge worked for the railways as an artisan, on the technical side, he then taught technical drawing at the Port Elizabeth Technical College in Port Elizabeth and then at Daniel Pienaar Technical School in Uitenhage. He continued teaching and farming after his mother, Elsabie, moved to Johannesburg and died in 1991.

The old homestead at Forest Glade.

Elvidge married Annette and had three children Charles, Yolandi and Charlene. Sadly Annette died young.

Elvidge remarried Lynette Kruger (nee Williams) in 2001, she had two children from her previous marriage: Mariennka and John-Ross.

Elvidge was only 59 when he died from a brain tumour in 2009. Lynette is now living on the farm with her daughter, Mariennka, and little grandson.

104. Gumdale.

Jenny Eldridge

The first occupant on Gumdale was a Mr. Muller, who is buried there.

Original homestead on Gumdale

Rupert Noel Whitehead (known as Noel) was born at Forest Glade in 1891 and went to school at Tip Tree, Forest Glade and Muir College. He moved to Gumdale in 1912 where he farmed wheat, fruit, vegetables, cattle, sheep and bees. He married Jacoba Ferreira (known as Kosie). They had three children: Rupert Frederick (1915-1926), Anthony and May. They lived in the old house that was built by the Mullers and in

1935 built the homestead that still stands today. The homestead is now used for church services.

After the death of Kosie, Noel remarried Prissilla van Niekerk and they had a son Eldridge (known as Elno) (born 1935).

May Whitehead:

May married Ruby Cohen and lived in Port Elizabeth.

Anthony Whitehead:

Anthony married Agnes Gertrude Pilcher (known as Bokkie). The farm was divided and Anthony got the portion Afdak. They had three children: Marlein, Noelin and Edwin. When Anthony died in 1991, the farm was passed to Bokkie's brother Dr. Deon Pilcher who practices in Port Elizabeth. He has wild antelope on his farm and facilities for overnight visitors in the lovely Lodge. His wife Alma is also a medical doctor who practices in Port Elizabeth. They had two children Leanie and Phillip.

After the death of Kosie, Noel remarried Pricilla van Niekerk and they had a son Eldridge (known as Elno) (born 1935).

Eldridge Elno Whitehead:

Elno went to Muir and then to Marlow where he studied agriculture. He met Susie Fourie from Kirkwood and they married in 1961. They built there present house above the road in 1961-62. Susie is a keen gardener and has a lovely garden. They had two children Sugnet (born 1963) and Colin (born 1966). * *Colin's poems appear a few pages on.*

Sugnet Whitehead:

Sugnet attended Nico Malan High School in Humansdorp and then to Wellington and Stellenbosch. She married Pier van Wyk in 1987 and they had two children: Pieter (born 1993) and Eldie (born 1998). Sugnet and Pier are very involved with the church and mission society.

The young Whiteheads in the late 1950's: Elno, Charles, John, David, Elmarie, Yvonne, Jenny, Marlene, Stephanie, Elvidge, Allan, Helene, Helen, Audrey.

Colin Whitehead:

Colin had muscular dystrophy from birth and was never able to walk. He was a true inspiration to everyone who knew him as he was always cheerful and never complained. He had an automatic little buggie and was able to get around the farm and town quite easily. Colin was secretary of the farmers' association for many years. Unfortunately he died in 2003 (aged 37) and it was a deep loss to everyone in the valley.

105. The Meadows.

Jenny Eldridge

The Meadows was bought round about 1922 by Frederick Whitehead (Senior) (known as Freddy) and was later given to his son Frederick (Junior) (born 1908). Freddy married Eliza Ineze Ferreira (born 1908) (known as Ineze). He was a very successful farmer and added on to the farm over the years. They lived in the old house but later built another house both of which are still being used today. They had three children: Lovemore (born 1930), John (born 1936) and Dawson (born 1943).

The Homestead at the Meadows

Lovemore married Rita Fourie had three children: Grego, Vincent and Fouche who all lived in Port Elizabeth.

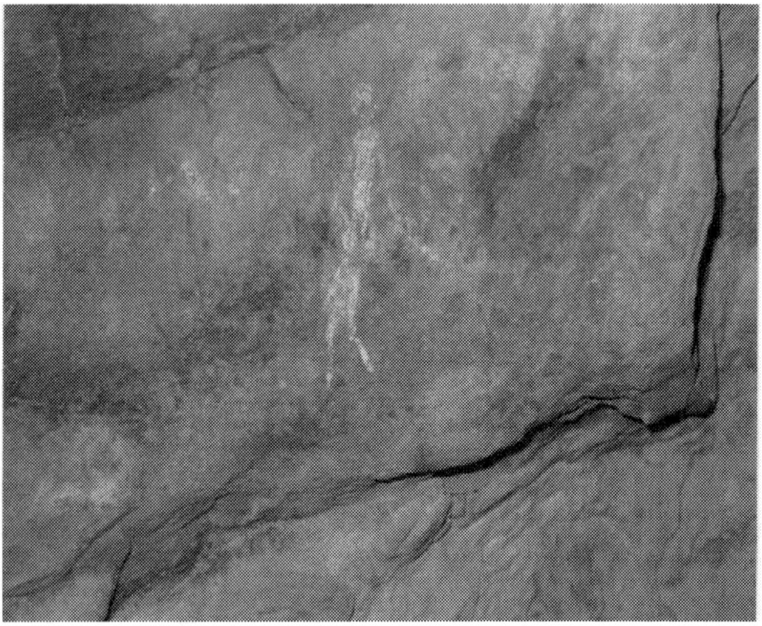

A Bushman Painting, in the mountains behind the Meadows. The painting indicates that bushman and white people came into contact all those years ago. Notice how the white image is clothed.

John married Joyce Strydom and had two children: Neil (born 1964) and Donavan (born 1966). John went to Brandwag and then to Marlow before coming to farm with his father. Neil is still a bachelor and Donavan married Franscina Jordaan (Senior). They had two children: Franscina (Junior) and Novan. Donavan and Franscina (Senior) divorced and Donavan remarried Sunelle Lamont who already had two children: Eduard and Stephan. John continued to farm until his death in 2006 (aged 70). The Meadows is now being farmed by his son Donovan.

Dawson became an art teacher in Port Elizabeth and later moved to Kimberly. He married Virginia Slabbert who was also a teacher. They had three children: Bevin, Mardo and Owen.

Freddie died in 1981 and Ineze in 1995.

106. Medicinal Plants found in the Elands River Valley used by the locals.

Jenny Eldridge

Perdepis – Horse wood – *Clausena anisata*:
Leaves and stalks are boiled and the infusion is used for coughs, colds and congestion.

Bitter Salie – Bitter leaf – *Brachylaena elliptica*:
Leaves are boiled and the infusion is used for lowering blood sugar, gargling and a mouthwash.

Bitteraalwyn – Bitter Aloe – *Aloe ferox*:
Leaves and roots are boiled and the infusion is used for worms, arthritis and a laxative. Aloe gel is also used commercially.

Wildeals – African wormwood – *Artemisia afra*:
Leaves are cooked for 5 minutes, honey is added and is used as an analgesic and an antihistamine as well as for coughs.

Balsemkopiva – *Bulbine frutescens*:
Sap is used for skin complaints such as burns, rashes, itches, ringworm and cracked lips.

Kooigoed – Everlasting – *Helichrysum odoratissimum*:
Smoke is used as a fumigant to repel insects and parasites. One can also use it when bathing.

Gaansie – Cancer bush – *Lessertia frutescens*:
Leaves are boiled and the infusion is used for stomach problems, internal cancer and to lower blood sugar.

107. Life on the Farm.

Nathan Oberholzer

I am now 15
and not at all that clean.
I ride my bike through the mud
and hence I know I am a STUD.

Everywhere I can go
and – Oh – never - ever - slow.
Up and down the mountains
in and out the fountains.

I have won a race or two
and will not stop till I do
win every race
at full pace.

I would love to do this all day
but sadly am in dismay
cos I have to go to school
as I know - I am still a FOOL.

108. All The People.

Nathan Oberholzer (Grade 9)

We are all different ladies and gents
Because we are not all so very urgent.
A few people are slow
And others are in fast mode.

We are all made of different colours
White, Black and Coloured.
It does not matter as they said
Because all our blood runs red.

We learn to live together
And when we get this right forever.
Will South Africa be a better place
For all the people of the different race.

109. Stan and Bert.

Cindy Oberholzer

To me, one of the pleasures in life is meeting new people. For the most part we meet people of similar stature, race and class. Then on occasions we meet people with personalities like dishwater, excruciatingly dull. But on the rare occasion, one is blessed with an absolute treat. Those people who leave you pondering life, and thinking about them for years to come.

On my travels, collecting these stories, a few locals told me about two brothers, Stan and Bert who lived like boemelaars, at the base of the Cockscomb. I had a preconceived idea of these 'bums' in the bush and what the hell were they thinking, living like this in the 21st century. My childlike pre-judgment concluded that they must be: poor, backwards and fools. So with much apprehension Adrian, my husband, and I paid them a visit.

On our arrival we explained what we were doing. They were friendly and keen to chat. So without hesitation they sat down, in the sheep kraal. Adrian followed suit. I first tried to find a spot where there was no sheep shit. Alas there wasn't a square centimeter unoccupied by a drol, so I gave up and just sat. I had forgotten when last I have sat, on the ground, on my bum. It's not that easy anymore.

My first impression was one of sadness and a desperate need to help them. I mean – "obviously" they needed help. They were skinny and the ingrained dirt appeared to have been there for years. Their clothes were meagre and thread bare. It was the middle of winter and just the week before, the Cockscomb was covered in snow. Stan was wearing thin material shorts and no shoes. Although, I must say, his top half was warmly covered.

I looked around, there wasn't very much, two small run down, make shift houses and a chicken hook. About 70 sheep, 5 cows and a handful of chickens. A tap - outside. No phones, no electricity, no bath, no hot water, no shoes, no car, no fridge, no bed – only a kooi, on the floor, with some sheep skins for blankets.

I asked: "What do you eat?"

They answered: "Food is not that important. We eat because we have to, so it's mealie meal in the morning and a potato at night. If there is some meat we put it in a pot and boil it up. But the meat goes off quickly, so mostly if we slag *(slaughter)* a sheep we make sheep biltong which we eat a lot. Sometimes we have a little coffee and the chickens give us some eggs."

"And how do you financially survive?"

"We each get a small pension from the Railways and Goodyear, which is enough. We don't need a lot. Every two months a guy from Uitenhage comes and fetches us, so we can buy a few things from town. We don't like to go to town, so we don't go if we don't have to."

Stan was very quiet but curiously observant, sitting there like a Meerkat, on the other hand Bert liked to talk, he talked and talked about politics and would quite often say: "Ask me. I know everything." Without saying a word Stan's shoulders would shake going up and down: "Giggle - Giggle."

Let me tell you a little about them:

Stan and Bert Rudman come from a large family, with 10 siblings, extremely hardworking, loving, humble family and yes, a family who had seen too many extreme hard times with absolutely no food or clothes and a meagre living.

Stan is now 77 years old and was born on this farm. He attended Primary school until Standard 6, at which point his father needed him on the farm so he stayed home to farm for the next 10 years. He then became "independent" and took on a job as a Jackal Hunter, for the next three years, where he earned himself R2 per jackal. He loved his job and was extremely good at it. He could scurry up and down the mountains like a dassie. He was at one with the bush. Thereafter he took on a "serious" job and for the next 20 years worked for the Railways as a Spanbaas *(Team leader)*. Although he settled down and bought himself a little house in Uitenhage, in the same street as his brother, Bert, he never did take a wife or have children, he remained a loner. He returned to the farm thereafter.

I said: "Stan – That would make you the most eligible bachelor in the Elands River!" Without hesitation his shoulders started to shake up and down: "Giggle – Giggle."
Then there is Bert who is now 82 years old and as a youngster was fortunate to attend high school in Patensie, after which he worked at Goodyear for the next 40 years. He took a wife, but never had any children. His wife had passed away many years ago and after a while he decided to come 'help' Stan on the farm. He had a strong opinion about politics, which will be wise for me not to repeat and reminded us often that he was there to look after Stan.

Sadly our time was up, we bid our farewell and in the car on the way home:

I said to Adrian: "How sad, they have no money."
He said: "How fortunate, they have no need for money."

I said: "They live like 'bums'."
He said: "They live like that by choice. Are we brave enough to choose?"

I said: "How difficult, they have no lights or stove."
He said: "They have the stars and moon for light and a fire to cook on."

I said: "They are alone."
He said: "But they are not lonely, they have been brothers, together, for 77 years."

I said: "They have no water."
He said: "They have a constant stream of fresh mountain water, flowing through their front yard."

I said: "They have such a little food."
He said: "That's why they are so healthy, they eat to live not live to eat."

I said: "They have no space in their house."
He said: "Their house is outside and it is as far as the eye can see."

I said: "They will leave no legacy."
He said: "How wonderful, that all they will leave is footprints – kaalvoet *(barefoot)* nogal!"

Cindy Oberholzer - Aka "The Fool"

P.S. That icy night, while we were cuddled up, spooning in our warm, soft bed, simultaneously we said: "I hope Stan and Bert are warm."

Stan and Bert's House

Bert Rudman

The most eligible bachelor – Stan Rudman

110. The Circle of Life.

Cindy Oberholzer

On our daily walk, we came across a dead teenage baboon, under the power line stays. He had sadly been shocked to death. One could clearly see the fur still on the electric cable, as well as his chest hairs had been frazzled.

The incident must have happened an hour or two earlier as he was fully intact, rigor mortis had not even set in yet. The ants had gathered in their droves, you could not stand too close, for being overrun and bitten by them.

We stood there, with a heavy heart, as we felt for this poor ill-fated baboon, what a fright he must have gotten - did he wake up this morning thinking this would be his fate before his breakfast - how was his mother and family holding up. All that effort, love, patience and hardship into this precious life – gone in a flash!

The baboon was in our thoughts, so the next day, our walk followed the same route, to see how he was doing. Well! What a fright we got as the entire body was covered in big fat juicy maggots. You could not see any of the baboon, for all the maggots. There were even areas moving back and forth as if alive, the way they crawled as one. I was absolutely dumb founded, to see that in 24 hours - flies had laid eggs – hatched – and big fat maggots were before me now. No – if anyone had told me this tale, I would have to google their "lie". Well, I had seen it with my own eyes, so it had to be truer than Google! I was mortified to think that all these thousands upon thousands of maggots would transform into flies and attend my next braai! I now cursed the dead baboon for ruining my next social, what would my friends think - when there are more flies at the braai than there are Chinese people!?!

The maggots were now in our thoughts, so the next day, our walk followed the same route, to see what they were up to. Well! What a fright we got as the entire body, maggots, bones en die julle bleddie lot, were gone. All that was left, was a flattened piece of veldt with a very – very – I repeat – very - bad smell. Sis – you could not breathe for wanting to puke. Before we could even make an assumption as to what happened, Spike, the Jack Russell, dove into the wrenching stench and rolled and rolled and we shrieked and shrieked and called and called him – too late - the dog now stank from ass to elbow.

On our walk home we came to the assumption that a Bosvark must have come across this platter of maggots and thought he won the Bosvark Lotto. Well he snacked the whole lot. Hell - can you imagine his breath the next morning.

By the time we sat down to lunch, that day. I felt more at ease with the circle of life. The sorrow I felt for the baboon had subsided. The anger I felt for the maggots, turning up uninvited to the next braai, had calmed and the gladness I felt that the Bosvark had cleaned up the mess, as well as received a hearty meal, pleased me.

Until - Spike darted into the house - jumped onto the couch and rolled around and around!

The circle of life – what a bitch!

111. The Sangoma's Powers.

Cindy Oberholzer

My husband and I were going overseas for two weeks. An exciting but daunting event. The kids and dogs were at their kind Aunty Jacqui and the farm was in the hands of our trusting 'estate manager', or more commonly known as the garden boy, Eric. He had been with us for a lifetime, although there had been ups and downs over the years, which is acceptable, as this is Africa. Adrian, in a moment of 'weakness', gave Eric the bakkie keys, with strict instructions of using it around the farm, as he normally did, and to wash it while we were away. When we drove away I commented on his braveness and contemplated his stupidity.

Two weeks passed in a flash and honestly thinking back I cannot even remember where we went but clearly remember our return!

Before the car door closed our 'assistant estate manager' came to us stuttering something along the lines of there has been an 'incident'! While the kids, dogs and bags piled out the car. The assistant estate manager continued, with well selected words - almost rehearsed, he told us that there had been an unfortunate incident with the bakkie and Eric was not at work today. After much beating around the bush, stuttering and repeating himself - thirty minutes later the 'spilt beans', where on my grass.

Eric had taken the bakkie, for a joy ride, to a local tavern and 'bumped' it. Adrian, trying to contain himself, briskly strolled to the garage only to find an absolutely shinning bakkie, which had been smashed squarely into a pole. The bonnet, windscreen and roof had a straight smash line running from bumper to roll bar. He must have hit the light pole squarely.

Adrian quickly realised that the 'assistant estate manager' had carefully left out the gory details such as: 1. The extent of the damage. 2. The relative soberness of Eric. 3. The quantity of passengers. 4. The level of stupidity.

Now - with heart valves being tested to the limits and flared nostrils, Adrian closing his eyes, breathing deeply and calmly asked: "Where is Eric?" The response: "He is at the Sangoma getting mootie. He knows you wouldn't fire him but he not so sure you wouldn't kill him!"

That was very powerful mootie as Eric is still alive and still working for us.

112. Believe It or Not.

Cindy Oberholzer

Adrian Oberholzer, from Tanglewood (Cypherfontein), had the most interesting and unique mother.

Her name was Pam Oberholzer, (neé Polhill), whose parents came from the upper classes of England. Although, when her father, Stanley, returned from the war, he returned to a broken England. No jobs, no money. Even the upper classes where in dismay. His eldest brother took over Howbury, the family estate, leaving the siblings with essentially nothing. He ultimately got a job on a farm in Kenya.

Hence a few years later Stanley's daughter, Pam, was born in Kenya. Pam blossomed into an elegant, slim, highly intelligent, elegant, beautiful women who possessed all the qualities of royalty, but from the word go Pam never fitted into normal, she was a "bush baby". She disliked being indoors and till her death, felt uneasy when there were walls around her. She spent her life in the bush, with her horse, Toska and her black companion, Kierwa. At that time a black companion was assigned to each child, to follow them and keep them safe. The three of them, Pam, Toska and Kierwa would go on safaris into the untamed Kenyan bush. Pam studied the bush, hunted lion, elephant and rhino.

When Pam was about 20 years old the families eyes were on the lookout for eligible suiters. This was not part of her plans. She ducked and dived every suggestion and meeting, but over time the family slowly wore her down, so when an invitation and boat tickets arrived to attend Prince Phillip's (yes Queen Elizabeth's husband) royal ball, back 'home' in England, Phillip had come of age and was to meet all the eligible ladies, she reluctantly agreed.

On the morning the family was due to leave, the household was in a flurry, with last minute preparations and packing. Stanley noticed his daughter was not amongst the flurry. On investigation of her room he found a note: "Father. Forgive me. I cannot meet Phillip. If he chooses me, I will be confined to a icy Castle, a prison, for the rest of my life. I will certainly die if I leave Africa."

When Stanley saw that Toska and Kierwa were also missing, he knew she was safe.
So instead of Pam arriving in England, a well worded, letter of apology explaining an unforeseen illness, disembarked in her place.

Pam, Toska and Kierwa returned two weeks later, with two buck.

It is now a family joke - when 'King Phillip' appears on TV, the families comment to Phillip is: "Unbeknown to you, Phillip, you settled for second best, when you married the Queen!"

113. The Orphan Child.

A Soloman Marais story retold by Jenny Eldridge

Soloman Esaias's (Solly's great-grandfather) eldest daughter Susanna Ferreira, who lived behind the Cockscomb, died giving birth to her son. Susanna Barnard (nee Marais) (Solly's great grand-mother) went over the mountain to collect the little boy and brought him back to their home at Bergplaas. They appropriately called him Hansie and he was raised as their own child.

114. Rokoptel.

A Soloman Marais story retold by Jenny Eldridge

The old road, which meandered above the dam at Solitude, was given the name "Rokoptel" (Lift your Dress). There are two versions as to the origins of this name.

The ox wagons crossed the stream at that point and the woman had to walk across having to lift their long dresses up high.

And an ox wagon, laden with apples, overturned at that point and the women gathered the apples using their skirts to hold them.

115. The Lifeline.

A Soloman Marais story retold by Jenny Eldridge

The lifeline to the Elands Valley was a railway bus, which came out once a week from Market Square Uitenhage. It went all the way up the valley to Melkhoutboom where the driver slept overnight. The bus brought the post, transported goods such as wheat and passengers.

116. The Spanish Donkeys.

A Soloman Marais story retold by Jenny Eldridge

The farmers in the valley used oxen and 'Spanish Donkeys' to plough the fields, pull wagons and scotch carts. These brown donkeys with white mouths were imported from Spain.

The road up the Valley was built using picks and shovels. The gravel was transported by scotch cart. The road to Patensie was built by the early settlers and the road to Steyterville by British soldiers during the Boer war. There was a British Garrison stationed at Melkhoutboom. While working on the road near Bergplaas a young white chap riding a Scotch cart with three Spanish Donkeys, was in a hurry to get past, so he threw a stone at the donkeys, this caused them to charge off, overturning the cart. He was flung from the cart and was severely injured and died shortly afterwards.

117. Poepbang.

A Soloman Marais story retold by Jenny Eldridge

Susanna (Solly's grandmother) told him of a man who was returning home on horseback one evening. While passing near Bergplaas, he saw a ghost. He and the horse got such a fright they both took off and only when they reached Bergplaas they stopped. He was in such a petrified state she had to pull him off the horse's back.

118. Missing the Moment.

A Soloman Marais story retold by Jenny Eldridge

On Bergplaas there was a zinc house, behind the present farmhouse, this was where the Marais' lived. Soloman and Susanna are buried in front of the house.

Hendrik Marais (Solly's father) also lived at Bergplaas after he married Cornelia Erasmus. The men would have to go to Uitenhage to get supplies for the farm. This trip took ten days. On one such occasion Hendrik returned and to his great delight, found his 5th child, a little girl, had been born. They named her Johanna Katarina.

119. Believe It or Not.

A Soloman Marais story retold by Jenny Eldridge

One day Hendrik Marais shot a Klipspringer up against the side of the mountain and when he went to retrieve the buck, he found two. The bullet has passed through the first, hit a stone and penetrated the stomach of the second!

120. After Eight Years.

Colin Whitehead (1995).

Colin had muscular dystrophy from birth and was never able to walk. He was a true inspiration to everyone who knew him as he was always cheerful and never complained.

It was the 10th October 1987, 4 o'clock they say.
For two, it was an exceptionally joyous day.

That morning there was a scurry and a commotion.
And every now and again arguing and tears of emotion.

That midday they stood before the married council like mice.
Trying to listen to the Ministers words of advice.
But alas nothing went in, even when he repeated it thrice.

That evening a party was held for all.
With great dancing and excitement in the hall.

Later grabbing the cheques and making a run.
Not even looking at the presents for fun.

To start their honeymoon for goodness sake.
As now they were wed Mr. and Mrs. "Van Wyk!"

We heard nothing of the honeymoon.
The sparkle was their good fortune.

Their innocence they would lose fast.
As being children was now in their past.

They first lived in Pretoria, but later moved.
To a place by the name of Dirkiesdorp.

Pierre's work brought him little thanks.
As he worked with people who were always drunk and tanked.

Sugnét helped out at the local school with supervision.
But received little money for her contribution.

She bought herself a spade, fork and gardening cans.
But along came little Pieter and froze all her plans.

She occasionally felt she could strangle the kid.
But one look from him and she melted instead.

Pierre, Sugnét and Pieter van Wyk, so true.
Nowhere is there anyone like you.

Tomorrow is the 10th of October you see.
A beautiful future we all see for you, so free.

Keep looking up to the man who steers.
And you will see your future clear.

Congratulations, your anniversary is in sight.
Remember it lasts till midnight.

121. My Grand Parents.

Colin Whitehead (1995)

Two Grandpas and Two Granny's were my life's key
Precious grandparents I know of no one so lucky.

My mother's father was Grandpa Jan
He was a very good man and such fun
Helped everyone under the sun.

He was first involved with building
Thereafter got involved in farming
Many admired him for his diverse skilling.

Granny Susie was my mothers, mother
God serving and full of love like no other
She occasionally lost her calmness
It was then best to move away from her hiss.

They left Kirkwood even though they were attached
To make their mark in Despatch
There they worked as an untiring team
To help everyone was their dream.

My fathers, father was Grandpa Noel
No problem was too big for his hardy soul
Gumdale kept him busy you see
Even when his legs were exhausted he stood like a tree.

Always a smile upon his face, a teasing
Especially when it was hunting season
Beaming smiles on hunting day
"Biltong is my absolute favourite." : he would say.

Granny Priscilla was my fathers, mother
No one moaned at all about her
As I must say I did not know her well
Just that she could smother you with love until you fell.

They forged a farm out of 'Gumdale' for us
Till today stands our house strong and vas
My grandparents live now in the Heavens house
I thank them for my parents and our homely house.

122. Our World.

Colin Whitehead (1995)

From Rocklands to the looming Hanekom
Lays a beautiful piece of land and then some
Beware, this part of the world can be damned
As although it may appear so, it is no lamb!

A hard world I hear
A place that can make you shed a tear
A place that entices you with its call
Even knowing you may lose it all!

The one who wants to farm here must know
Forget about riches as you sow
Here you have to pace your money and respectfully treat
To ensure you always have a little something to eat.

Exceptional people farm here
Even though occasionally we have to look of fear
Early to rise and no sitting around
Otherwise desperations is what will be found.

Everyone works together here
For a better existence to eliminate a tear
Occasionally there is the odd misunderstanding
Ultimately we all live in good standing.

A view over the valley.

Here is where we will stay forever, like an immovable tree
Cause here is where we all feel free
From the worlds bickering and rush
There is solice in feeding the chickens their daily crush.

We are filled with joy and pleasure
Fortunate to be part of this treasure
I will not swop it for all the money
As the Elands River is sweet like honey.

123. Life.

Colin Whitehead (1995)

Life is a funny thing
The unknown, is what it holds within
Sometimes it makes no sense
Nasty, it can jump on you in the present tense.

Most lives are dedicated to just making money
This occasionally does the exact opposite, that's so funny
As it often leads to turmoil and unrest
Remember life is not solely a money test.

You're rich and think you're on top
Life often makes a bow, my friend, a full stop
You never think you'll fall from this sky
But tomorrow you will look them in the eye.

Many disabled cannot work and one hears their sobs
However many do, in fact, have great jobs
Do not think of their bodies weak or strong
Reasons to strike are many and wrong.

All is what we want to buy
The neighbours also have and try
Many believe money is the only hope
But love is free, not a penny it costs, oh nope.

Love has no monetary value, you see
Here on earth it's absolutely free
From children to the aged, I shout
Even if you're down and out.

For every women and man
Life has its own plan
Even though it seems we do not know
The best way forward is as a team we sow.

Occasionally life is a strenuous fight!
Give these troubles over to Jesus's full might
Before him we can always plead
For mercy to stand us in good stead.

Do you search for a life with good luck?
Are you under a heavy burden stuck?
Turn to Jesus, he's there for you and me
Away will float your burdens free.

124. Time.

Colin Whitehead (1995)

Ever wonder: "What is time"?

This is what buggers us around
For eternity this will be our hound
For all our worldly turmoil and troubles
I wonder, are we managing our time muddles?

Time has no colour or taste
But yet it's time that rules our daily haste
Everyone is at its mercy and command
As it's what tells us when what is in demand.

Time is money, so it's said
More time, more time it's our daily bread
No matter how fast you walk or run
24 hours is all a day will give, which is not fun.

Time can make you wait, this is its might
No matter if it is day or night
Time can make you chase your tail
Do not test it, it will make you frail.

Once gone there is no getting it back
Lost time can make you bitter and lose track
Use your time as a wise treasure
Then you will be certain of life pleasures.

Your life's time is pre measured
This is a gift, to be treasured
How long till the end of our wow's?
You see, its God who decides and knows.

125. Un-Understandable?

Colin Whitehead (1996)

Humans are impossible to understand
This is echoed by almost all man
This matter is extremely contra-versable
As people are un-understandable.

Instead of constantly arguments being fanned
And concentrate on making a better land
Many want to strike for more pay
And not see that others' lives, lay in dismay!

With the one hand man kills
With the other he asks for meals
Unrest lies on the other side of dread
Rather work harder for your daily bread.

It feels great to indulge in a little skinner
But caution my friend, this is not a winner
If you've nothing nice to say, say nothing at all
As tomorrow you may need their help to still stand tall!

Helpful, Honesty and Kindness
On occasions one thinks these are useless
But give it a little time
In the end it's these that make things just fine.

That's why man is un-understandable
As all of life's, life-able
Lays in God's caring hands
This is clear and Understandable.

126. Meals!

Colin Whitehead (1996)

We sit and eat our 'brekvis'
It's pap and jam - oh yus what I lus
I tell this is no farce
Fun for all is forecast.

As the clock strikes one, it's is the big deal
Come stand a little closer, you seal
Look, a feast upon the table for our meal
Oh - hunger in this house, you will never feel.

Dinner is as exciting
One never knows what mother will bring
Does not matter what's in that thing
It's always yummy and worth a tasting.

While I am bragging
The best of all – no it's not my belly sagging
Is in my comforting knowledge
There's nothing like meal times under the 'Gumdale' foliage.

127. Like a Bird.

Colin Whitehead (1996)

From goggas to people and every creature in between
We all have the exact same wish this is foreseen
Healthy bodies and a tummy, full inside
It's such a pity, on occasions there is a divide.

All lives consist of ups and downs
Sometimes it's as if it's doing the rounds
For others it's like rocks, full of discontent
Yes, there is no exception, no one is exempt.

I wish I were a bird, so free
To glide and slide, so for a day I am not me
And as the wind passes through my feathers
It washes all my molecules leaving all untethered.

As I look up into the free sky
To watch a bird sway and fly
Suddenly my wish is a joke
You see there's a falcon giving me, the bird, a stoke!

Does life make any sense
As issues surround you, in every tense
Remember, God got you this far
He has a reason, a purpose, he knows you're a star.

As Jesus lives within us all
He enables us to stand real tall
Stick to the plan, the one Jesus has for you and me
Your happiness will soar, like my bird, so free.

128. We.

Colin Whitehead (1996)

Married in Nineteen Sixty One
At Gumdale they committed to each other, under the sun
Today is Nineteen Ninety Six
The years I have known them thirty, it's true no tricks.

My "ABC" my mother taught me indeed
While in Humansdorp my sister got on with her studies
In hospital I still did my lessons, said mother said she
While the doctors toiled over my legs you see.

A healthy child I was not and health care was not for free
So my father went to work at GKV
To send me to Kimberley
Off to attend a school called Elizabeth Conradie.

My sister studied in Wellington
They taught youngsters to live without sin
Via post I persisted till eventually with no tricks
I qualified, Yahoo, in Electronics.

Through all the years my family
Shared lots of fun, laughs so lovingly
Still as one, all our kin
This all through the grace of God within.

For our family of four held much power
All the years of sweet and sour
But ultimately it's been an absolute pleasure I tally
On our farm in the Elands River Valley.

My sister no longer lives with us
She now has her own family over which to fuss
It does not matter what the future holds
As they walk with Jesus through life as it unfolds.

From day one of my life's journey
The Lord has been my rock, joined to me
I could not have done it without this family
Always at the ready to give their love so steady.

Thank you Lord for my family.

129. My Parents

Colin Whitehead (1996)

I thank the Lord for my parents so kind
Precious parents you will not easily find
Nothing could get me down or flustering
As alongside me they stood unwavering.

To a normal school, I could not attend
As off to hospital regularly I'd go to mend
With love you stood by me without fear
Sometimes with a laugh, sometimes with a tear.

Protecting me against the most horrible issues
Which without you, would've required a mountain of tissues
All the while helping me to better understand
The Lord, You and I against all could withstand.

My father's heart into the land he did throw
Although ultimately worked for 'Geustro'
You see my illness ate at their pockets, leacher
Without a moan my mother was my nurse and school teacher.

Forever I will remember you
To me and Sugnét you were eternally true
Parents of note they were true Pro's
Our Parents: Susie and Elno.

Susie and Elno Whitehead outside their house

130. My Dear, Dear Friend!

Colin Whitehead (1997)

Another life, is with what I daily tussle
Against many things I must struggle
A life no one can understand for their bustle.

Much asking: "Why me?"
This life makes me mad you see
And then I realise how privileged I am, which is key.

Cindy Oberholzer

At my school, I have seen, a very sad case
A friend of mine who will never reach the adulthood space
But yet always a smile upon his face.

In 1978 he could still walk ahead
In 1984 we lost him to the dead
Till the end, his concern for others led.

He thought me one thing and that was to be sturdy
Never to be bothered by condescending 'buddies'
But instead to dedicate oneself to study.

Books were his first lover
They were in fact his dove
As he and his homework fitted like a glove.

He was like a brother to me
A friend by my side, which set me free
An anchor he was, a steadfast tree.

The Lord was his soul mate
He gave him strength to live in this state
As he knew exactly his ends fate.

His was my proof, till the last day
No matter what your lives fray
Jesus will show you the way!

Thank you. Thank you, you are now my martyr!
You now rest in heaven, with someone a lot smarter
My Dear, Dear Friend: Allan Parker.

131. Off Too Hospital!

Colin Whitehead (1997)

You must be off, to the hospital you go
There is a problem your doctor says it is so
Off to lay in a hospital ward
Where daily you pay as if a hotel lord.

Oh a non-responsibility form you must sign - you must
And then in your doctor you can trust
That all will be well it guaranteed it's for certain
There is nothing hiding behind the small print it's not a curtain.

There's nothing to fear
We'll be cutting deep into your flesh
While the doctor reads deep into your history
This fills you with death's mystery.

Then you are called
You are washed and overhauled
Even new places are washed and discovered
Especially where they'll be cutting, are mothered.

Cindy Oberholzer

With a trolley you arrive at the operating table
Where you lie with a cloth the size of a label
The bright lights shine above you, that's who
Leaning over a masked monster, who wants to devour you.

You feel the pricks upon your skin mount
With this the doctor tells you, you must count
Say good bye to your conscious world pray tell
From this sleep world you awaken only to feel like hell.

Prehaps it's not necessary for an operation
Just a sickness that needs medication
For recovery, they do not give you a long time
As others behind you, for your bed, stand in line.

Yip, it's a place of death and life
Here one receives heart sore, joy or strife
For some their sickness's will lead to the end
For the defensively new born, a mother who will easily defend.

No matter if you are kind, old or hated
No matter what's wrong or to whom you are related
This place makes you feel incredibly on edge
One holds on for a kind word to talk you off that ledge.

Whether you are an outpatient
Or whether you are a private patient
At some point or another, we will all stay in this place
When it comes to health issues, no exceptions, we all must face.

One must give all at the hospital a second thought
As they care for everyone and this cannot be taught
24 Hour service without fail, that's correct
To all involved for my care you have my utmost respect.

132. The Law?

Colin Whitehead (1997)

Our Land has a new law
It goes by the name of the Land Law
Offered to everyone, riches, happiness and fun
Before we had to work for everything to be done.

Through lawlessness our country is run
We are now by theft and murder overrun
Many have out of desperation immigrated
And are compelled to return by the force of migration.

The only law that'll solve this problem. Is who?
It's calling out from Mathews 22
Just as Jesus's love is abundant and unclean
There will be no injustices that will go unseen.

How come is it that we do not want to forgive each other?
Jesus gave us his life - like a mother
All our sins have been forgiven - forever
Come, let us live life and love together.

With Jesus on our side we can find
Build, for all of us, in mind
To take each other, with love, by the hand
To germinate trust and nutrition into this land.

133. Crossword Puzzle?

Colin Whitehead (1997)

A puzzle of blocks and questions like a maze
One will be kept pondering for days
Some are left bewildering
The blocks constantly heralding.

A word for a word you search diligently
Next to you, every kind of dictionary
And when the answer doesn't come, you curse - out loud
Oh hell - you now feel so unproud.

I am sure many words are made up for frustration
This only infuriates the situation
Oh hell, what does one now do
To find a fellow word that's true?

While you sit and watch The News
From the bedroom your wife calls out: "Excuse me who."
"Help me to choose an appropriate word"
You give a suggestion and she calls out: "That's absurd!"

If you want to win a little money
Many will think you coocoo or funny
In the end it's up to just you and your pen
No one is coming to answer. Across – number 10.

Do not be one who does dismay
If you cannot get it, it's likely no one may
There's easy one's for you and me
The answers eventually come – you'll see.

134. The Value of Money – 1804.

Vol 1, Elands News, publisher Colin Whitehead (2002)

The monetary system of 1804 was very different to today. It consisted of eight coins. They were:

Value	£	s	d
Doubloon	4	0	0
Johanna	2	0	0
Guinea	1	2	0
Ducaton	0	9	6
Pagoda	0	8	0
Spanish Dollar	0	5	0
English Shilling	0	1	0
Copper Coin	0	0	2

135. The Keurkloof Ghost.

Elno Whitehead

During 1928 the Bulk and Sand River dam walls were heightened Uncle Koedoe van Niekerk worked at the Bulk River and boarded at my father, Noel. He had a fancy for a girl at the Sand River, whom he used to visit.

One night he lent my father's horse and went to visit his sweetheart. On his way back, near Keurkloof, he had to stop and open a gate. He noticed someone standing at the gate. He called out and asked for them to open the gate. He received no response, so he climbed off the horse to open the gate himself. When he pushed the gate, it swung right through the person. He got such a fright he jumped on his horse and hauled it out of there.

Around the same time Ralph Billson, a plumber working at the Sand River, also met with the same ghost.

One night Ralph was on his way to the Sand River, when his Chev motor started to overheat. He stopped around Keurkloof to get some water from the stream. When he was heading back to his car, he saw someone standing at the car. He called out: "Can you help?" but there was no reaction. He was a little frustrated with the insolence of the stranger and when he got closer he swung his water bottle at the person only to have the waterbottle pass right through them. He got such a fright he jumped in his car and sped off without filling it with water.

136. The Doctor who Nearly Did Not Become a Doctor!

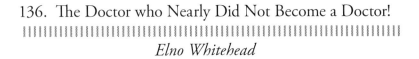

Elno Whitehead

During the building of the dam at the Bulk River Oldman Lewies Ofsowitz owned the shop. He was responsible in foreseeing that the workers were provided with supplies. Lewies had 3 sons, Solly was the baby of the lot.

Solly and his wife were shopping in Uitenhage to stock the store. On their way back Mrs. Ofsowitz lay her baby, Solly, on the floor of the horse drawn cart, to sleep. When they arrived home, Baby Solly was gone. They turned back in the dark, to search for Solly, they found him at Grootnek (were the rondavel house stands today). Baby Solly was miraculously not injured, however according to the tracks on the ground the horse cart wheel had just missed his head.

Baby Solly later became the honourable Dr. Solly Ofsowitz, serving the Uitenhage and it surrounds.

P.S. Dr. Ofsowitz was the first doctor to service the valley, later doctors were Dr. Jacques Snyman, Dr. Solly Ferreira and Dr. Jannie Snyman.

137. Interesting Facts about the Wild Life.

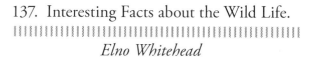

Elno Whitehead

Most of the wild life found during the 1700's and 1800's in the Western Cape was also found here. This is also where the Valley gets its name from, as Eland were found here. Some of the first whites who established themselves in the Gamtoos Valley and came over the Elands Burg mountains to hunt in the Elands River Valley. According to my research, the last Eland were spotted around 1776 – 1778.

An interesting fact is that the last Black Rhino was shot on the farm Echodale, which at a time was owned by Allan Frost.

I could not establish when the last Elephants were sighted, however there are signs of a watering hole hollowed out by them, on a ridge, on George Whitehead's farm, Mountain View.

Of all the wildlife which survived the Valley the longest was the Buffalo. The last one was shot at Buffelskop in the lower Elands River Valley.

The last troop of Wild Dogs were poisoned with a poisoned mule, by the Rautenbachs on their farm Doornhoek in the 1800's.

Other wild life shot out were the Oribi at Uitkyk during 1930.

The last Grey Rhebuck was shot at The Bulk River around 1938.

138. The Arrival.

Elno Whitehead

Through the years the Valley has been hit hard with numerous floods, which obviously created much destruction and dismay.

The flood of 1981 was the worst in the last 100 years, the Valley thus had the highest recorded water levels.

Uncle Sampie Rautenbach's, from Cypherfontein, roadway washed away and he was stuck on the farm. His sister-in-law was due to visit them for the holidays and Sampie was to fetch her from the airport. When she arrived at the airport there was no one to fetch her. She tried to make contact, however the phones were down. She coincidently started chatting to an air force pilot about the situation in the Elands River Valley. As it so turned out he was about to do an inspection of the Valley and invited her to come along for the ride.

Great was the surprise, for the now panicking Uncle Sampie and Aunty Johanna, when a helicopter landed in front of their house and out climbed their guest.

139. Tragedy.

Elno Whitehead

During the floods of 1983 a tragedy occurred when one of the Wehmeyer's, from the farm The Fonteine, workers wanted to cross the river and sadly drowned.

140. The Tourists Drama.

Elno Whitehead

During the floods of December 1970 a certain Mr. and Mrs. Ealdon with their 3 children, were making their way through the Elands River Valley, from England and on their way to Uganda.

They had disembarked off a ship in Durban and by car toured South Africa. When they arrived in Port Elizabeth they decided to experience the beautiful Elands River Valley. While traveling up the valley they encountered a storm and by the time they came across the Sand River crossing, the river had washed the road away. They had to turn around and head back, however by the time they got to the Bulk River the road had also been washed away.

There they sat for one day and one night, with nothing to eat or drink. The Monday morning they came to me for help, they had to catch the boat in Cape Town to return to England.

After we gave them dry clothes and a plate of food we returned to their car at the Bulk River. We realised that their little car would not make it through. That afternoon we went to look again. The water had subsided a little. We then decided to attach their little car to my bakkie and just pull them through.

When we reached the other side, coincidently there was a reporter who took our photo and listened to our story. The following day we were on the front page of the Herald.

141. Come Fetch your Ox.

Elno Whitehead

During the floods of 1950, Uncle Abram van Niekerk's oxen, who were grazing at the time on Uncle Freddie Whiteheads farm, were washed away. Three months after the flood some people went to catch eel near Rocky Valley and to their surprise, between two valleys, was an island and trapped on the island was one ox. He'd survived on bulrushes and reeds. A special road way had to be made in order to get him out.

142. The Snake that nearly Caused Chaos.

Elno Whitehead

Before the arrival of the tractor, ploughing was done with oxen. Wheat was sown by hand and sickles were used to reap the ripe wheat. Bundles were made by hand. When the entire field was in bundles, the bundles were loaded onto a trailer and packed into 'hay' stacks close to the threshing machine where they would wait their turn to be processed.

While the last bundle of wheat was being loaded onto the trailer a cobra shot out from under the pile. The cobra began striking at the oxen. After we killed the snake, we called it a day and went home immediately. We unspun the oxen and herded them into the kraal, where we watched and waited to see how many would die from the bite. After about an hour, nothing happened. We were dumbstruck. We went back to the snake, perhaps we had miss identified it. We were correct it was a cobra, however to our surprise in the cobra's mouth was a half swallowed skaapsteeker. How fortunate for us, the cobra could not get a good tooth bite in, as his mouth was already full.

143. The Ghost that Unspan Oxen.

Elno Whitehead

(This story was told to Elno by Uncle Sampie Rautenbach who stayed at Cypherfontein (Now Tanglewood), Sampie passed away quite a few years ago.)

The farmer's produce was transported to the Uitenhage market by ox wagen. The unspanning was done at Graskop, where the ox wagons would stop for the night. Early in the morning, still in the darkness, the wagons would be spanned in again to continue the journey.

From Graskop there was a long downhill, were the oxen had little to do, however this was followed by a steep uphill. So when the oxen began to pull, it was discovered that the oxen had been unspanned. The wagon drivers dreaded this stretch, as it was extremely difficult to fix the mess that followed after everything went rolling in every direction.

144. The First Settlers in the Lower Parts of the Elands River Valley.

Elno Whitehead

Charles Mackay, a City councillor in Port Elizabeth, settled at Rocklands. A historic city council meeting was held at Mountain View, to discuss the building of the Sand River and Bulk River Dams. (Two of his great grandchildren, Jenny Eldridge and Allan Whitehead, still live on the farm).

Richard Tee came from Norfolk to the Cape in 1819 and in 1844 he bought the farm Boschfontein for £ 450, from Phillip Frost. The farm measured 3000 morgen and had 4 homesteads on it, making it four complete farms. Richard settled at Holl River in 1853. One of his descendants Denzil Desmond Tee, still owns and lives on the farm.

Vivian Tee and Sylvia Doyle who are also related to Richard Tee, farmed for many years on the farm, Welcome Home, before moving to Uitenhage.

Sidney Whitehead (Frederick Whitehead's brother) bought part of the farm Boschfontein where he farmed for many years. His son Lyall farmed in Uitenhage, where to the present day, Penford, is. Lyall had a big vineyard and made wine and brandy as well as a dairy to supply the town with milk.

Izak Abraham van Niekerk settled on the farm Stilgenoeg in 1850, he had 8 children. His son, Pieter, was the father of Waldo, Naas, De Wet and Hannes, who were all well known in the Valley.

Alexander farmed on the farm Orange Grove. His son, Koedoe van Niekerk was a well-known garage owner in Uitenhage. Alexander's daughter, Christina, married Ignatius Minne and their grandson Aubrey Minne farmed on Rufordskloof before moving to Uitenhage.

Sussanna married Antonie Ferreira who farmed at Uitkyk and their daughter Susara Jacoba married Noel Whitehead.

145. The Baviaan – iaan.

Cindy Oberholzer - regailing some tales from a friend called Tuis

While visiting a friend, Tuis, who lives in the Baviaans, I mentioned the Elands book, which lead to him regaling a few Baviaans stories.

***

Tuis owns Sederkloof Lodge and employs a colourful, coloured guy, who goes by the name of - Kiwiet.

Kiwiet is indigenous to the area and can trace his ancestry back to the Dassie.

Tuis saw his potential and with a bit of English coaching and a trial run with Tuis pretending to be the guest, Kiwiet took him into the bush and give him the speal. Kiwiet passed with flying colours and from then on, he was entrusted with a new task, of being a bush guide for the guests.

Tuis explained: "Kiwiet, it is imperative that you do not lie to the guests. If you don't know something say – "I don't know"".

After Kiwiet's first outing, Tuis anxiously asked: "So Kiwiet, how did it go? Did you lie?"

With a shocked expression: "Haai - Nee - Nooit Meneer. Ek het baie naby aan die waarheid gebly." *(Oh – No – Never Sir. I stayed very close to the truth).*

***

When Tuis was building Sederkloof Lodge, he employed a builder from the area, his name Martin Gripphils.

One morning Martin come to Tuis, looking a little worse for wear, suffering from a hangover.
He asked: "Mister, have you got a little regmaakertjie for me, please?"

Tuis fully understood and gave him a beer.

Tuis curiously asked: "Martin. I don't understand. You are a respected man in the community. You are a Deacon in the Church. How then?"

Martin's reply: "Mister. A donkey has four legs and he stumbles. It is unrealistic that I, with my two legs, will never stumble?"

***

On our walk with Kiwiet he explained: "To cure a cold, you need to crush a wild dagga leaf with a eucalyptus leaf and then you add a bit of 'be-leaf' (belief). Hot water. Stir. Drink. Then you will be better.

***

Kiwiet regaled the story of his predecessor, Jakkals, who took a group of foreigners out on a bush walk.

In the group was a women, who asked questions - non stop! On the way up the kloof he painstakingly stopping at every bush and animal dropping to explain how, who, why, when and where. Even with his detailed explanations she asked more questions. The 2 hour walk turned into a 4 hour walk.
They came across a bush pig latrine, which created much excitement and the women kept them there for over 20 minutes, with every question about poo you could imagine.

By the end of the 'up' walk, Jakkals was now gatvol of talking, he was looking forward to the walk back, which normally was done in silence, as everyone just absorbed the surroundings and silence.

This was not to be. She cranked it up a notch. The net result was somewhere between the Dassie's Cliff and the Wild Dagga Boom, Jakkals lost his sense of humour.

So, by the time they passed the bush pig latrine again, he was finished. She started: "What ...?"

Jakkals, spun around, looked her in the eye and blurted, out: "Ag Tog Lady! It's just a pile of SHIT!"

146. Wattle trees in South Africa.

Cindy Oberholzer.

While John van der Plank was in Australia, he noted how well the Wattle Trees grew and decided to put a few seeds in a match box, which he brought to South Africa.

At its peak, wattle covered over 700 000 acres in South Africa and the exports of wattle extracts and wattle bark during the 1950's was valued in excess of £6 million.

In conversations with Danie Ferreira he recalled as a schoolboy one of his tasks, after school, would be to walk through the ploughed fields and sow wattle seed, which his father bought by the 20kg bag from Oubaas Lewies Ofsowitz, at the local shop.

147. Letter to a Mother – 14 January 1944.

George Whitehead (Senior). Based in Egypt during World War II.

No. 580750
Gnr. Whitehead
128th Battery
43rd Light A.A. Regt
U.D.F
M.E.F
14th Jan, 1944

My dearest Mother

At the present moment I am reposing on my bed in a tent which is being relentlessly beaten about by the wind. A small paraffin lamp which has been made out of a cigarette tin is supplying the necessary light but the naked flame is being disturbed by a breeze which is entering the tent and consequently it is flickering incessantly. While I am writing my tent mates are amusing themselves with reading to the onlooker. We would seem a very comfortable and satisfied four but I can assure Mum that one can see changing faces when the word "guard" is mentioned as it is a very wild night. My half-section is going on guard now. I wish that Mum could see him crawling into warm clothing. He has just shouted those words to the one he has to go and relieve "Is it cold chicken." I may add that it is darn cold and I am thinking of my beat at 12 O'Clock tonight. The weather has really been miserable today and the wind is still blowing. We had a few drops of rain this afternoon which served the purpose of damping the surface of the sand so preventing an unpleasant sandstorm. It really gets terribly cold up here during winter, especially at night. I suppose that summer will soon be here again and then we will experience intense heat in addition to the violent sandstorms which come at that time of the year.

Today it is just four months ago that we arrived here in Egypt and it really seems like a year. Time seems to pass very, very slowly up here.

How is Hilda, Ned and Baby getting on these days? I wrote to her on the 12th of last month but have had no reply up to the present. Has Mum found out whether Tony ever received my letter which I dispatched about four months ago? Please let me know as I am patiently awaiting a reply. It was really tragic to hear about the plane crash in which Andrew Jordaan lost his life. I had often seen him while I was still at Muir and he was really a strapping young man. Please give my regards to Norman and sister Susy and ask Norman how the girls are getting on in Uitenhage. Also remind Dad that I am looking forward to receiving a letter from him.

Well Mum, I suppose I had better draw to an end now as I have no more news except that I am still in the peak of health.
With tons of love to Dad, Stan, Mum and the rest.

From your loving son.
George

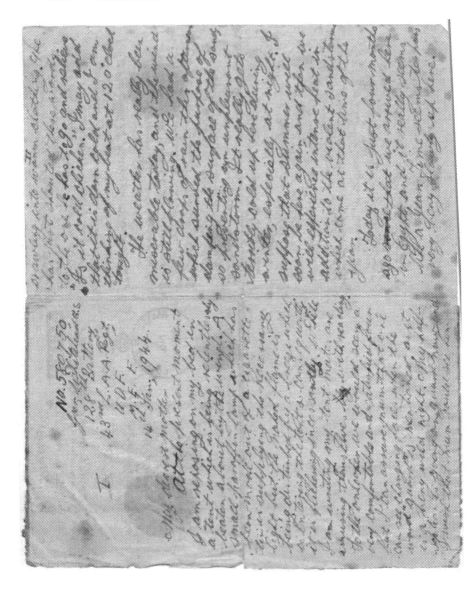

148. Letter to a Mother – 17 January 1944.

George Whitehead (Senior). Based in Egypt during World War II.

No. 580750
Gnr. Whitehead
128th Battery
43rd Light A.A. Regt
U.D.F
M.E.F
17th Jan, 1944

My dearest Mother,

Many thanks for your loving letter dated 5th Jan which I received last night. It was quite a relief to receive the letter as I had not heard from home for over a week.

I was indeed glad to hear that both Mum and Dad were having such an enjoyable holiday at Amsterdamhoek and I sincerely hope that you will both benefit by the change. It was indeed a strange occurrence when the bee stung little Charles. Tell Hilda that he is destined to become a bee farmer if he can stand a sting at such a young age.

The weather improved somewhat yesterday and we had the privilege of experiencing a calm and sunny Sunday. However the change has not succeeded in lasting and today the wind is beating over the sands again. I may also add that we are still experiencing bitter cold during the nights. The moon has once more waxed to full and shines with brilliance on the desert sands at night.

I have not seen Micky for some time. The last time we met he told me that his Mom had mentioned the fact that there were hundreds of people camping at Jeffrey's Bay during the Christmas holidays.

Thanks ever so much for sending me Dollies address as I must write and thank her for the parcel. Please write and tell me whether Aunt Priscilla received my letter. Tell Dad that I am beginning to give up hope of ever receiving a letter from him. I hope the rest will supply him with some extra energy so that he won't feel to tired for writing at night. Has Mum heard whether Tony succeeded in passing his 2nd years B.Sc. exams with honours? Please try and find out whether he too received my letter.

I suppose that I will find quite a changed farm when I arrive home someday D.V. especially the new homestead which Stanley is having built.

I have been digging about in the sand like a rabbit today but I cannot disclose the purpose of the digging. All I can add is that it was not very pleasant digging while the wind was howling the sand about at the same time.

Well Mum, I will have to draw to a close now as news is scarce.
With tons of love to all at home and may God bless you all.

From
Your loving Son
George

149. Letter to a Mother – 24 Febuary 1944.

George Whitehead (Senior). Based in Egypt during World War II.

No. 580750
Gnr. Whitehead G.S
128th Battery
43rd L.A.A. Regt (V) S.A.A.F
U.D.F M.E.F
24th Feb 1944

My Dearest Mother

Well here I am again just to drop you a few lines and to tell you all that I am still keeping in the best of health.

To my great disappointment I did not receive a letter from home this week. I can assure Mum that I am beginning to look forward to mail with far greater eagerness these days on account of your illness. I can assure Mum that I have been worrying a great deal ever since I received the bad news, never the less I am hoping for the best and be assured that you are always remembered by me in prayer.

We have had the pleasure of enjoying very favourable weather during the past few days, and I can give the assurance that this change in the weather has been fully appreciated owing to the most miserable days experienced last week. Monday night was perfect but I must admit that my thoughts were centred entirely on home as I gazed at the scores of bright stars which were twinkling incessantly from the bluest of skies. It reminded me

of the happy nights spent among the valleys and the mountains of Mountain View, where I was reared in an atmosphere which causes me to become a lover of nature. There are many days that I long for those precipitous kloofs, the peaked mountains and the deep blue lagoons. This barren Desert forms a striking contrast to my home but I must admit that it also possesses its charms.

Last night I had the opportunity of seeing a concert which was presented by an U.D.F. entertainment party. It was really a good concert and I thoroughly enjoyed the evening. Needless to say laughter was again one of the main features as far as the spectators were concerned.

I have regret in announcing that Micky is in Hospital. Another friend of mine has been in hospital for over a month.

Well mum, I will have to draw to a close now as I have no more news except that I am keeping in the best of health.

With tons of love to Mum and Dad and may God bless you dear mother.

From
Your loving Son
George

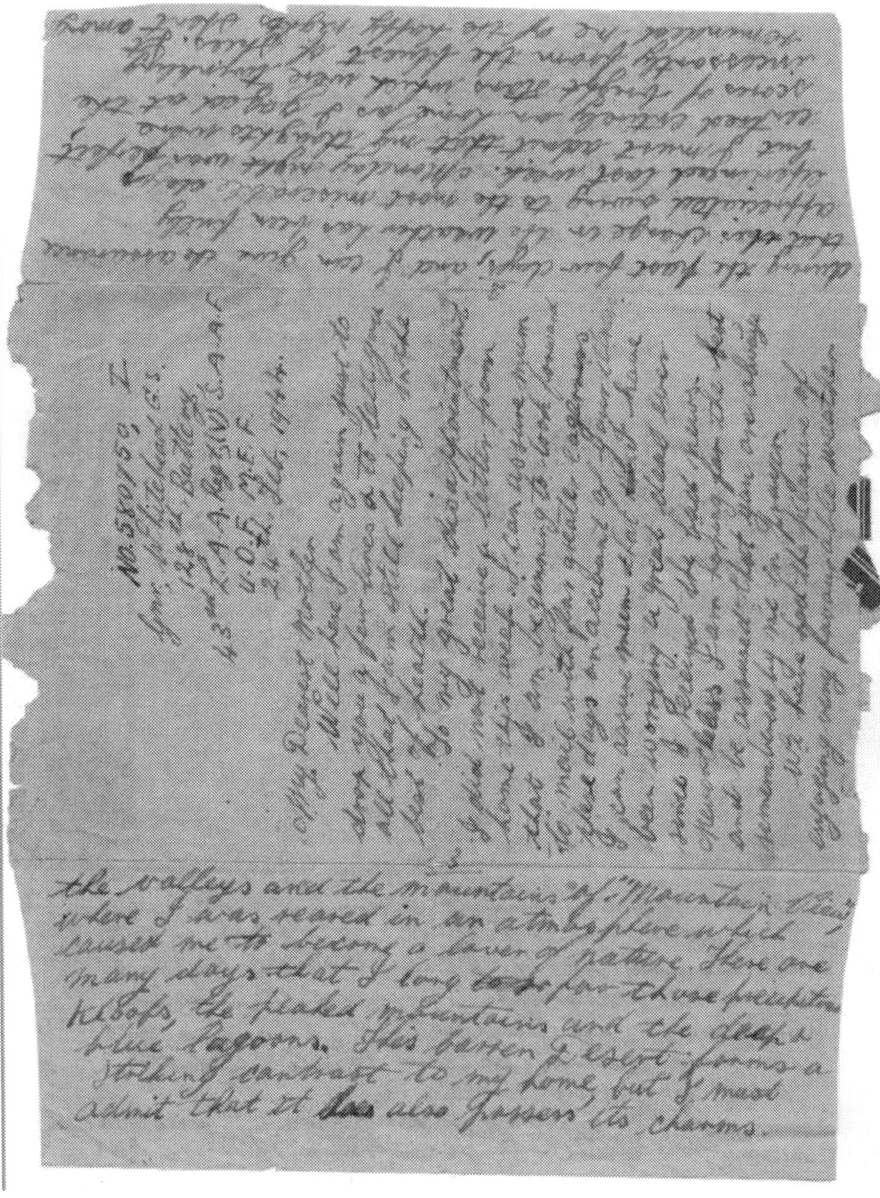
the valleys and the mountains of "Mountain View"
where I was reared in an atmosphere which
caused me to become a lover of nature. There are
many days that I long [illegible] for those precipitous
knobs, the peaked mountains and the deep
blue lagoons. This barren desert forms a
striking contrast to my home but I must
admit that it [illegible] also possess its charms.

150. Letter to a Mother – 15 May 1945.

George Whitehead (Senior). Based in Egypt during World War II.

No. 580750
PTO. Whitehead G
"D. boy"
FC/C.T.H.
6th Armd. Div
U.D.F./C/M/F.
15th May 1945

My Dearest Mother

Your loving letter dated the 3rd to hand for which ever so many thanks dear. I was indeed sorry to hear that Dad is having such trouble with his teeth. I wish he will make up his mind and have the whole lot out.

Well I had a very pleasant surprise two days ago when I received two parcels – one from Mom and the other from Hilda. Thanks a million. Mom, I can assure you that I enjoyed and am enjoying every single item of its contents. Unfortunately the figs had gone mouldy, but that is just due to the long period of travel.

I can well imagine what excitement prevailed among you folks when you received the good news about Italy. No wonder the phone kept on ringing. Yes the beastly often had been terribly whipped by our armies and had they not surrendered they would have been completely annihilated. Those bomb-happy ones that managed to escape death. I had been through it all with my regiment, but I wouldn't like to mention anything as yet. When one has been in battle and seen the slaughter one wants to forget. My platoon commander which was an officer loved by his men, was one of the many friends that lost their lives in the early stages of offensive. He was only 23 and was such a determined and inspiring leader.

We are having very hot weather of late and the days are amazingly long. It gets light at five and one can read a book up to 9.30 at night. However we are living in comparative luxury these days so nothing can really worry us. There just seems to be that urgent desire to get home. But we must just have patience.

With all my love and thank Dad for the few welcome lines. God bless and good luck.

Your loving Son
George

No. 580750 V
Pte. [illegible]
"D" Coy,
F.C./C.T.H.
6th Armd. Div.
U.D.F./C.M.F.
15th May 1945

My Dearest Mother,
Your loving letter dated the 2nd to hand for which [illegible] so many thanks dear. I was indeed sorry to hear that Dad is having such trouble with his teeth. I wish he will make up his mind & have the whole lot out.

Well I had a very pleasant surprise two days ago when I received two parcels — one from mom & the other from [illegible]. Thanks a million mom. I can assure you that I enjoyed & am enjoying every single item of the contents. Unfortunately the figs had gone mouldy but that is just due to the long period of transit.

I can well imagine what excitement prevailed among you folks when you received the good news about Italy. No wonder the phone kept on ringing. For the beastly Hun had been terribly whipped by our armies & had they not surrendered they would have been completely annihilated. Those lucky ones that managed to escape death. I had been through it all with my regiment but I wouldn't like to mention anything as yet. When one has been in battle & seen the [illegible]

151. Letter to a Mother – 6 January 1946.

George Whitehead (Senior)

No 380750.V.
PTE. Whitehead, G.S.
6th Jan '46

Dearest Mother

Your loving letters dated on 12th and 20th to hand, for with ever so many thanks dear. I was indeed glad to learn that your folks were still keeping in good health. Actually I received your letters three days ago, but owing to a suspicious scent in the desert air I refrained from answering immediately. I first wanted to conduct further investigation and now I have obtained sufficient evidence to hang the murderer. So please don't be angry with me for having missed the mail bag. Here are the facts in brief.

About 400 of us "H" group fellows will be leaving by boat on the 9th, inst. D.V. I am not sure whether we will sail on the same day but we are scheduled to embark on this date. The boat will in all probability dock at Durban so I will have a nice long train journey to look forward to. However I will soon be on my way after landing in Durban so there is nothing to be perturbed about. If everything goes "plain sailing" I should be enjoying Moms good cooking by the 27th inst, D.V. I can well imagine how pleased Mom will be at my sailing instead of flying, although I would prefer the latter. I will most probably wire you folks from Durban when I leave there. But I want no large gathering of relatives, nor any crying. Just bring the home circle along. This is a sincere request so please don't disappoint.

Well dearest news is no longer necessary so you can pack the old pen away. This will be my last letter to be written from Egypt. By the time this reaches you I will be well on my way to S.A. sailing the blues. The next time you will hear anything from me will be when I shout for some more coffee. D.V.

With all my love and best wishes. May God bless dear ones, so cheers till we meet again. This is the letter I have for a long time been cherishing to write.

Love

George

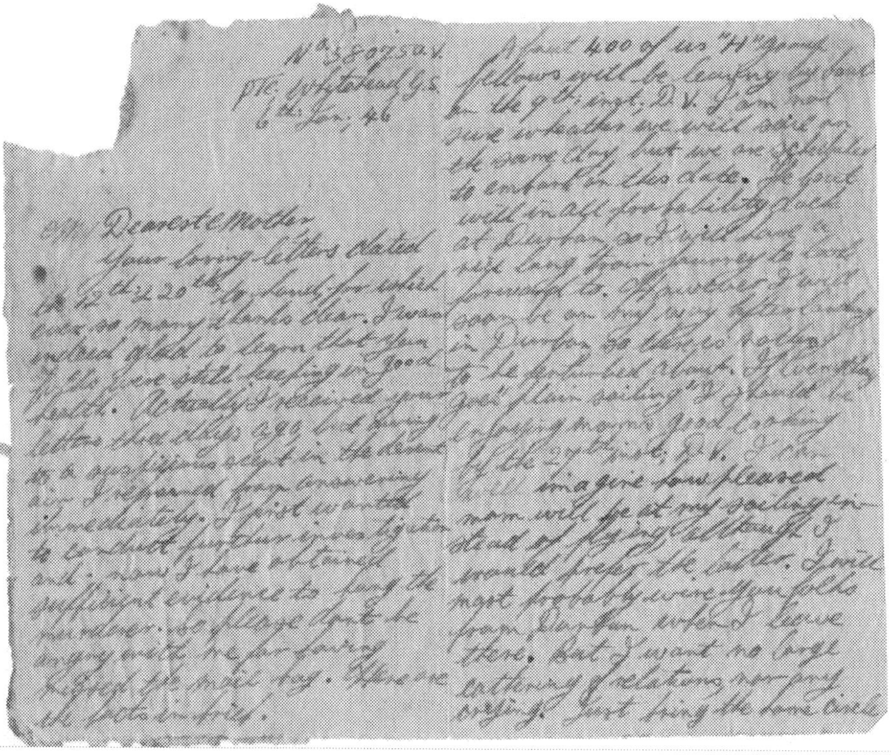

No. [illegible]
Pte. Whitehead G. [illegible]
6th Jan, 46

My Dearest Mother
Your loving letters dated the 12th & 20th to hand, for which ever so many thanks dear. I was indeed glad to learn that you & all were still keeping in good health. Actually I received your letters three days ago but having [illegible] I refrained from answering immediately. I first wanted to conduct further investigation and now I have obtained sufficient evidence to [illegible] So please don't be angry with me for [illegible] boy. [illegible]

About 400 of us [illegible] fellows will be leaving by boat on the 9th inst. D.V. I am not sure whether we will sail on the same day but we are scheduled to embark on this date. The boat will in all probability call at Durban and I will [illegible] from Durban to [illegible] Anyway I will soon be on my way [illegible] in [illegible] If everything goes "plain sailing" I should be enjoying mama's good cooking by the [illegible] D.V. [illegible] imagine how pleased [illegible] will be at my sailing instead of flying although I would prefer the latter. I will most probably wire you folks from Durban when I leave there, but I want no large gathering of relations nor any crying. Just bring the home circle

152. The Lawyers Bill.

Whitehead, Mountain View 13.11.1936

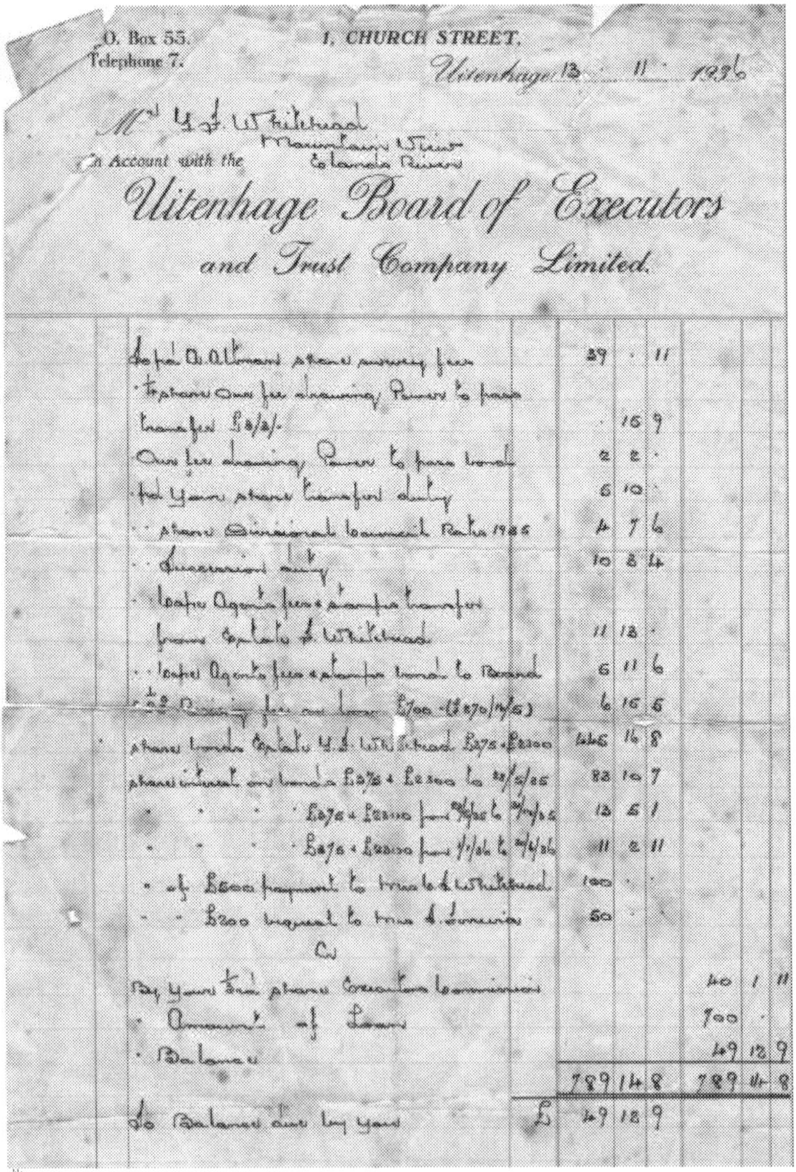

.O. Box 55.
Telephone 7.

1, CHURCH STREET,

Uitenhage 13 . 11 . 1936

Mr Y. J. Whitehead
Mountain View
Coleraine River

In Account with the

Uitenhage Board of Executors
and Trust Company Limited.

	39 . 11		
transfer £3/3/-	15 9		
	2 2 .		
	6 10 .		
	4 7 6		
	10 8 4		
	11 13 .		
	6 11 6		
	6 15 5		
	446 16 8		
	83 10 7		
	13 5 1		
	11 2 11		
	100 . .		
	50		
Cr			
		40 1 11	
		700 . .	
Balance		49 18 9	
	789 14 8	789 14 8	
To Balance due by you	£ 49 18 9		

153. Did you know?

Cindy Oberholzer

28 July 1914 to 11 November 1918 – World War I

1 September 1939 to 2 September 1945 – World War II

154. Elands River.

Jessyca Whibley

A valley of strong men, as the mighty mountain terrains.

Women of gentle kindness like the loving summer rains.

The sun kissed children run through the fields of lucerne and clover.

A land that is mysteriously, cruel and kind in a day.

Fight it and you will walk among the bones of your life stock with a heavy heart.

Go with the flow of hope and the rain will pour and the land will sing.

This echoes from the land, neighbours and animals.

Respect thy neighbour, respect the land and live in harmony with mother earth as she intends us all to.

155. Places to Stay & Things to do.

Cindy Oberholzer

The Elands River Valley has become a spectacular tourist destination for the bush lovers – so below find places to stay or things to do. Note: contact details and facilities may change over time, its best to check first.

Kammievlei

Self catering accomodation, 4 bedroom, sleeps 10, house to rent.
Contact: Beer (Roelie) or Sareta Beer, 082 569 1914
beertrek@mweb.co.za

Sand River Getaway

Tented chalets, fully kitted kitchen, pool, hiking, small functions/weddings and boma area.
Contact: Colleen 082 748 4903
info@sandrivergetaway.co.za

Off Camber Adventures

Chalets, camping, 4 x 4'ing, pool, quad hire, team building, hiking, small functions and boma area.

Llisa Dodd – Artist - Hillingdon

Llisa Dodd is a renowned, all round, artist. She specialises in landscape (acrylic) as well as various medium commisions. Llisa also gives art classes and judges competitions. Contact: Llisa Dodd, 076 282 3953
llisedodd68@gmail.com

Mount Ingwe

Self catering house, chalet, 4 wheelers, 4 x 4'ing and a must see personal Anglo Boer War Museum.
www.mountingwe.co.za

Burrows
Self catering log house and hiking.
Contact: Tinus Vermaak

Landela
Accomodation and entertainment for christian and group camps. Sleeps 64.

The Meadows
Tracks for 4 x 4'ing and day visitors.
Contact: Sunell Whitehead, 082 458 9580

Mountain View
Chalets, camping and hiking.
Contact: Geoge Whitehead 082 900 1201

Indigenous tree nursery.
Contact: Jenny Eldridge, 084 327 9702

Wistaria
Organic food farmers.
Contact: Melani and Robin Volker.

Melkhoutboom
Cheese making
Contact: Rolf and Liezel Clotz

156. A Last Word from the Compiler/Editor/Author.

Cindy Oberholzer

I've learned so much while writing this book and am richer for it. I've met some interesting people, seen some unusual places and experienced some unusual feelings. I was humbled to learn about courage, poverty, humour and kindness, beyond measure. I only hope that you too, pause to digest the predicaments of these past souls and reflect for a moment. "But by the grace of God, that could have been me". For me history is not about dates, places and facts. It is about our everyday lives. This is the history that matters, when one can feel, imagine and empathise with old souls.

My first intention was to only have stories of the Valley, however, along came some great historical snippits, poems and stories from our neighbours, which just had to be added.

My apologies: To anyone I did not get to. My apologies also extends to any incorrect historical facts I may have unintentionally made. My intentions were always good and based on the information I had to work with. I tried to honor the style of the creative writings I received with the respect it deserved, even though it wasn't always grammatically correct.

Thank you: To all who shared their stories, photos and parts of their lives with me. A special Thank You to the late Danie Ferreira. Your stories are the foundation of this book. Thank you to Llise Dodd for the magnificent front and back covers. Your art inspires me, as it feels like the Valley. Thank you to George Whitehead (Junior) for nudging me on. Thank you to Cindy Irvine, Jeannette Goodman (English version), Talitha Kotze, Llise Dodd and Maria Dodd (Afrikaans version) for the proof reading of this book. Thank you to my family, who on many occasions ate egg on toast for supper, due to my time constraints.

A warning to all who settle in the Valley. Before you know it, the Valley has a way of seeping in through your feet, making its way up your spine and settles in your heart. Well then, putting it bluntly, you're buggered.

When reflecting on what I am still in awe of with regards to the Elands River Valley, it would be: **"The Space of Silence"**.

157. A Little About the Author.

Cindy was born and raised in Port Elizabeth, South Africa. Her family moved to the Elands River Valley (approx. 1 hour from Port Elizabeth) around 2006, where they farm with sheep and cattle. They also own a Fibreglass Manufacturing business, in Port Elizabeth, which takes up most of their time.

She has a newly married daughter, Jessyca 25 yrs old and a son Nathan 23 yrs old. Her cats, Toulouse and Miss Macaroon, have now taken their place.

While chatting to her, about the book, she was amused that while at school, she got an E for English and an E for Afrikaans. Writing a book was for everyone else, not her. She rightfully noted: "As one gets older you realise you have a choice to believe the perceived restrictions imposed on you by others or not."

Cindy Oberholzer

158. Elands River Rainfall - Mark Dodd - Hillingdon

Rainchart from 1994 to 2018

	Jan	Feb	March	April	May	June	July	Aug	Sept	Oct	Nov	Dec	Total
1994	40	65.5	85.5	32	24	33	61	111	51	50.5	17	112.5	683
1995	84	34.5	116	64	45	6	3.5	45.5	56	32	114	87	687.5
1996	69.5	16	46	12	9	0	47	54	50	243.5	270	138	955
1997	49	29.5	48.5	221.5	81	81	33	53.5	35	55	36.5	18	741.5
1998	80	22	131	29	23	11	20.5	98	52	29.5	69.5	82	647.5
1999	41.5	22	34	72	34	4	118.5	11	80	98	14	59	588
2000	127	109.5	161.5	85	4	4	13	5	38	65.5	133	46	791.5
2001	108	19.5	26	35	5.5	22	53.5	105	114	58	131.5	42.5	720.5
2002	47	34	23	26	57	36	147.5	210	83	13	51	60	787.5
2003	45.5	40	83.5	53	118	20	25	41.5	17.5	60.5	14	49	567.5
2004	39	88.5	60.5	30	16.5	35.5	30	13	115	81	16	204	729
2005	60	64	73.5	62	58.5	18	6	14.5	11.5	14	120	42	544
2006	103.5	58.5	32	85.5	178.5	41	25	321	48	49.5	50	67	1060
2007	32	22	201.5	38	124	10.5	27.5	43	9	73.5	44.5	114	739.5
2008	82	53	54.5	72.5	20.5	41.5	11	33	10	148	153	68	747
2009	27.5	66	19	51	46.5	89	100	16.5	32	91	28	36.5	603
2010	77.5	65.5	42.5	100	10	97	28	18	16	145	24	80.5	704
2011	51	39.5	42.5	57.5	148	202	100.5	37.5	7.5	48.5	63.5	60	858
2012	35.5	130	149	27	12.5	106	176	50	60	312.5	8	36	1102
2013	13.5	40	86	28.5	38	75	31	34.5	3.5	150.5	124	65.5	690
2014	32	41.5	71	117.5	14	28.5	6.5	57	111.5	21	92	68	660.5
2015	40.5	63.5	73	127	21	105	119	65.5	106	34.5	139	13	907
2016	31	36.5	58	27.5	35	20.5	82.5	18.5	67.5	34.5	45	21	477.5
2017	45	39	27	44	42	0	19.5	122	61	58	78	26	561.5
2018	29	66.5	49.5	11	23.5	11	20	71	159.5	36.5	55.5	19	552
Ave	55.62	50.66	71.78	60.34	47.56	45.7	52.2	66	55.78	80.14	75.64	724.2	724.2

Printed in the United States
By Bookmasters